the stepparent's survival guide

A WORKBOOK FOR CREATING A HAPPY BLENDED FAMILY

SUZEN J. ZIEGAHN, PH.D.

NEW HARBINGER PUBLICATIONS, INC.

Publisher's Note

This publication is designed to provide accurate and authoritative information in regard to the subject matter covered. It is sold with the understanding that the publisher is not engaged in rendering psychological, financial, legal, or other professional services. If expert assistance or counseling is needed, the services of a competent professional should be sought.

Distributed in the U.S.A. by Publishers Group West; in Canada by Raincoast Books; in Great Britain by Hi Marketing, Ltd.; in South Africa by Real Books, Ltd.; in Australia by Boobook; and in New Zealand by Tandem Press.

Copyright © 2002 by Suzen J. Ziegahn
New Harbinger Publications, Inc.
5674 Shattuck Avenue
Oakland, CA 94609

Cover design by Salmon Studios
Edited by Carole Honeychurch
Text design by Tracy Powell-Carlson

ISBN 1-57224-305-8 Paperback

New Harbinger Publications' Web site address: www.newharbinger.com

04   03   02

10   9   8   7   6   5   4   3   2   1

First printing

Contents

Part 1
The Stepfamily Dynamic

Part 2
Building and Maintaining Your Stepfamily Plan

Part 1

The Stepfamily Dynamic

Introduction

My Welcome to You

Welcome to *The Stepparent's Survival Guide*! You are embarking on a journey through the jungle of the stepfamily, and all of the wonderful yet challenging issues that will confront you there. I am pleased that you have joined other stepfamilies in the quest for knowledge that will help you plan ahead for problems and conflicts that inevitably face stepparents, biological parents, and stepchildren today. We will be exploring everything from the various types of stepfamilies today to the complicated and sensitive conflicts that you will face in your stepfamily, in addition to developing a Stepfamily Plan that will help you actually plan and build your stepfamily for the future. So let's discuss some of the specifics of the book and learn just how to use this valuable tool to help your stepfamily be the best it can be.

There are a variety of stepfamilies in the world today and I have attempted to make my book as inclusive as possible of all of these different formations. My hope is that you will identify with one of the types of stepfamilies discussed in detail in the book, understanding that your stepfamily may resemble others out there and finding comfort in knowing that you are not alone in struggling with the issues that stepfamilies confront. If the makeup of your stepfamily is very different from the types discussed in the book, I invite you to contact me and let me know. I am delighted to explore the many varieties of stepfamilies out there. The information and discovery benefits anyone of us involved in stepfamilies and performing in the role of "stepparent."

Also, I want to take this moment to discuss the terminology that I use in *The Stepparent's Survival Guide*. In the book, I use the terms "stepparent" and "stepchild." You will also see the term "bioparent," which I use to refer to biological parents in the stepfamily. Depending upon the type of stepfamily that you are living in, one adult will be the stepparent and one will be the bioparent. However, if you both have children, then you will both perform in dual roles—that of stepparent and bioparent.

Avoid Feeling Left Out

In my work with stepfamilies over the years, one main theme has appeared time and time again with stepparents having difficulty making the adjustment to the stepfamily. This theme is the phenomenon of stepparents feeling they have little to no control over their role in the stepfamily. Now, what does this mean, "little to no control"? By the nature of the dynamics of a stepfamily, two adults fill their roles in a stepfamily but a discrepancy soon reveals itself that doesn't occur in traditional families. This discrepancy is the inability for both adults to be equal in sharing *all* responsibilities in the stepfamily. Which responsibilities are difficult to be shared? Well, that's easy. It comes down to the parenting and decision making for the stepfamily as it affects the stepchild. Why? Because the stepchild is the offspring of only one adult in the stepfamily—which automatically creates a crevasse between the two adults' roles and responsibilities. At times this crevasse can be useful, such as when a stepparent may wish to withdraw from involvement with the stepchild. However, over time, this crevasse becomes wider and deeper, particularly if the stepparent is having difficulty bonding with the stepchild or if the biological parent is having difficulty "letting the stepparent in" and sharing the parenting and decision making that affects their child. A stepparent can then feel insignificant in this stepfamily while struggling with what role they really do play in the family. If this feeling is not addressed, it can escalate. Before stepparents realize it, they can feel quite alienated and isolated from the rest of the stepfamily members. Ultimately, this can be the beginning of the stepfamily breakdown.

So what can a stepparent do to avoid this from happening in their family? You've already taken the first step, which is to begin reading and working through this book. The main focus of the book is the Stepfamily Plan, and this plan is based on a stepparent's need to be *proactive* and to *plan ahead*.

Learning to Be Proactive In Your Stepfamily

One of the best ways to prevent feeling isolated, inadequate, or insignificant in your stepfamily is to take a proactive position. By acting proactively, you gain a position in your stepfamily where you can feel equal and fully involved. By taking a proactive stance in your step-family, you will be asserting your role in the family while simultaneously accepting the responsibilities that go with this. You will be claiming a strong position in your stepfamily and helping to create and build a long-lasting and healthy stepfamily that is successful and fun to be part of.

What does taking a proactive position mean, and how will it benefit you? Being *proactive* means being involved before the actual process of change. What does this mean in a stepfamily? If you are proactive in your role as stepparent, you become involved in the decision-making processes of the stepfamily *before* any change takes place—that is, before the day-to-day workings of the stepfamily set in and become established without your input. Being proactive allows you to be involved with decision making in the stepfamily right from the very beginning—which is where you should begin your involvement. After all, you are the other adult, parent, authority figure, and significant partner in a new marriage and a new family.

Stepparents have long taken the role of being on the back burner or in second place. This is how stepparents often feel once they realize what being a stepparent really entails, and this isn't a pleasant or acceptable feeling for many. Stepparents have long been expected to take a secondary role when it comes to their stepchild. There are some valid reasons for this, but there are also strategies that you can employ to allow the stepchild to be first while you simultaneously maintain a position of authority in the stepfamily, something that I feel is absolutely necessary in order for a stepparent to feel whole and significant in their step-families. Feeling second has long been associated with being a stepparent, and it's time that feeling changes—for the sake of stepparents everywhere and involved in any type of stepfamily. Stepparents provide a vital and fulfilling role in stepfamilies, and by learning to take a proactive approach in your stepfamily, you can avoid the unnecessary feelings of helplessness and hopelessness that so many stepparents have felt when confronted with being on the back burner and not knowing what to do about it.

Planning Ahead

In *The Stepparent's Survival Guide* you will also learn how to plan ahead for many challenges that you will face in the stepfamily. Planning ahead is a good strategy to adopt in a stepfamily. Why? Because there are many opportunities where planning ahead in a stepfamily can prevent the familiar and common feelings of anxiety, resentment, questioning whether marrying into this stepfamily was a good idea, alienation, and isolation that so many stepparents find themselves facing. As I was writing this introduction, I talked with a stepparent who confided that she spent her stepchild's teenage years locked in her bedroom when the stepchildren visited! This is just one example of what can happen to a stepparent if no planning takes place prior to the marriage and particularly if little to no planning takes place prior to merging related and nonrelated people into a new situation called a stepfamily. There are bound to be problems, concerns, conflicts, and incidents that will affect you in ways you had never imagined.

In this book, you will often read about planning ahead and how this will benefit you in your role as stepparent. Planning ahead can be one of the best prevention techniques in a stepfamily and is the basis for the Stepfamily Plan, which you will work through in this book. At every stage, you will learn suggestions on *what* to plan ahead for and *how* to plan ahead, based on input from your stepfamily members. Being proactive and planning ahead are keys to being a successful stepparent. These two key issues alone can help cement your position in the new stepfamily while simultaneously allowing you to avoid the emotional pitfalls that so many stepparents face and, up until now, had little information on how to deal with. But now *The Stepparent's Survival Guide* is here, and you have taken the proactive step toward the success of your role as stepparent by deciding to read this book and follow through on the exercises while building your Stepfamily Plan with your family members.

What You Will Encounter in *The Stepparent's Survival Guide*

In this book you will learn about a variety of issues including how your stepfamily measures up to other stepfamilies, the myths and realities of stepparenting, and the power of your beliefs about stepparenting. This background data is important to you because it provides a personal portfolio of information for you on how you view your stepfamily individually and in comparison to other stepfamilies. This will help you put your stepfamily situation in perspective. For example, is the conflict you're dealing with as serious as you perceive it to be or, in relation to other stepfamilies, is the conflict you're facing relatively common? Knowing this information can ease your burden and simultaneously decrease your stress by reassuring you that you are not alone. The key to the Stepfamily Plan is to not only provide you with information about what conflicts you will face but also to offer solutions that may work for you and that you can start using today.

Let's discuss my role in *The Stepparent's Survival Guide*. I am writing this book for you; so I can share my experiences with you and other stepparents in an effort to help you:

- pinpoint any specific concerns you have

- enjoy a calm and smooth journey into stepparenting, and

- to help you define your specific concerns related just to your stepfamily and understand how to resolve these toward building an effective Stepfamily Plan

I also wrote this book to help you know that you, as the stepparent, are a vitally important member of your stepfamily. You need to understand this about your role. In my work, I have found that stepparents feel a variety of emotions that are similar across the board, no matter what type of stepfamily you are in. These emotions and issues include feeling:

- that, by choosing the role of stepparent, they have given up their own identity and become lost in their stepfamily;

- second best or that they are placed on the back burner;

- that their opinions and desires for the stepfamily are often not taken seriously;

- that they need to adjust to their spouse and stepchild's way of family life without recognition for their own routines;

- that they become invisible in the stepfamily;

- they are overwhelmed and drowning in conflict;

- that they "lose" much of the time;

- they must compete with their stepchild for attention and acknowledgment;

- insecure much of the time in the stepfamily.

To get a feel for the book and how it works, let's jump in and do the first exercise.

Exercise: Explore Your Emotions at this Point

How are you feeling in your role? You can use the preceding list to help clarify your thoughts and add any additional emotions you may be feeling. Complete the following statement: In my role as stepparent, I have been feeling _____

_____

_____

Briefly indicate why you have been feeling this way. _____

_____

_____

_____

Now consider what one thing you can do to change how you feel. _____

_____

_____

_____

Whether you're feeling positive or negative emotions in your role right now, write this down in this exercise. Beginning to explore your feelings about being a stepparent is the first step to take with *The Stepparent's Survival Guide* and a great start to building your Stepfamily Plan.

Okay, Here Is Your Stepfamily Plan

You are in one of the toughest jobs that you will ever encounter. There is no job description for being a stepparent. But there are plenty of performance evaluations for the position. *Everyone* in the stepfamily seems to be evaluating you at each juncture in this journey. Like everyone else, stepparents are molded and shaped by life experience. Sometimes that life experience in a stepfamily can be joyful, but it can also be disappointing to the point where you want to quit this job and start over doing something else. This book is for you as a stepparent, to help you understand that you *can* have input into decision making for your stepfamily and that you truly can control your destiny in the family. This book will help you create your own job description customized to your individual stepfamily.

The book is structured into two parts. "The Stepfamily Dynamic" gives you background on conflicts and dynamics in stepfamilies to help you understand common themes. This information will help you put issues in your stepfamily in perspective prior to building your Stepfamily Plan.

The second part is "Building and Maintaining Your Stepfamily Plan." What is the Stepfamily Plan? The Stepfamily Plan is the step-by-step plan you create with the info in this book, knowing what to do and what not to do in your stepfamily to reduce or avoid common mistakes that lead to the breakdown of stepfamilies. The Stepfamily Plan is your opportunity to *plan* your stepfamily every step of the way.

In the pages that follow is your Stepfamily Plan. This is your personal, guided tour toward building a successful stepfamily. In this plan you will have a special view into conflicts stepfamilies face, *and* you will have the added benefit of knowing how to avoid and/or prevent the havoc these conflicts cause. You will be privy to knowing in advance what the pitfalls are that stepfamilies struggle with and how to plan for these pitfalls so that the impact on your stepfamily is significantly reduced. *The Stepparent's Survival Guide* is like having the test answers right in front of you, laid out for you to successfully pass the test.

So, let's take the test. What is this Stepfamily Plan, and how do you use it? I developed The Stepfamily Plan because I discovered in my work that stepfamilies were created with ease, but many were floundering, not knowing what their role was or how they were supposed to function. Stepfamilies were unclear of what direction they were headed in. It's like planning a driving trip across the country but doing it without a road map. Stepfamilies appeared to be living in chaos and ultimate confusion about what they were to do once the conflicts started. Few solutions seemed available. I started to wonder how stepfamilies would function with a plan—a well-thought-out and guided plan that required input from each member of the stepfamily on decisions and the direction the stepfamily wanted to take and what each member *wanted their stepfamily to look like*. I wondered if it would be possible for stepfamilies to know the conflicts in advance, plan ahead to confront and resolve them, and in the process, build a resilient marriage and stepfamily? The Stepfamily Plan is based on the knowledge I've gained over the years in working with stepfamilies on how to build stronger bonds in spite of the numerous conflicts and unpredictable difficulties that come up. Many of the conflicts stepfamilies face are similar; it seems only logical that these conflicts should be shared with one another. You may be experiencing similar difficulties in your stepfamily as one of the case histories presented here, and relating to that unknown but familiar family may help you learn what you can do to help you and your stepfamily and give you some insight into not only how to survive in a stepfamily, but how to help your stepfamily thrive.

The Stepfamily Plan is designed around the conflicts that stepfamilies face. These conflicts are detailed for you in the following chapters. You may be able to identify with one or all of the conflicts. I provide information about why the conflict occurs and what to expect when it does. You will also find information on how to deal with the conflict and plan ahead of time for this conflict to prevent any unnecessary disappointments, hurt feelings, or resentments. Preventing these emotions that eat away at the core of your stepfamily will help you and your stepfamily enjoy a continued bonding experience, hopefully one that is not wrought with frequent and deep-rooted tension and emotional upset. By following this plan, you and your stepfamily members will have more control over the fate of your stepfamily. You will be able to command the helm of your stepfamily's future, and not let your future guide you.

Stages of the Stepfamily Plan

The book is designed around the stages that stepparents will go through in their stepfamilies. I have designed the stages of the book based on my work with stepfamilies over the years, and I've found that most families face obstacles in the order in which they appear here. This structure is the basis for the Stepfamily Plan. By working through each stage, one at a time, and in the order in which you may face the issue, your Stepfamily Plan will be created through your efforts in planning ahead and building a plan for how to confront and deal with each issue.

Here are the stages of the Stepfamily Plan:

- Stage 1: Make Peace with Your Stepfamily's Past and Create Your Parenting Team

- Stage 2: Observe, Listen, and Learn to Control Alienation

- Stage 3: Assert Your Role in Your Stepfamily in Discipline and Other Areas

- Stage 4: Navigate the Extended–Family Member Circuit

- Stage 5: Be Certain Your Marriage Can Survive

- Stage 6: Examine Where You Still Need Work

- Stage 7: Maintain Your Stepfamily

- Stage 8: Create Your Stepfamily Traditions

Build a Stepfamily History

Each section provides case histories and exercises for you and your stepfamily members to complete. Because *The Stepparent's Survival Guide* is designed in a workbook style that you can take home and start using today, pages are provided for you to write information specific to your stepfamily. A Quick Summary is provided at the end of each chapter to help you evaluate at a glance how your stepfamily is doing in the areas discussed in the preceding chapter. You will have an opportunity to completely analyze and understand how your stepfamily functions in a variety of situations. At the end of each chapter, you will be provided with journal pages for you to detail your thoughts, plan your next steps, or to record information about your stepfamily. It's essential that you record your thoughts as you build your Stepfamily Plan, as this recording will help you create your stepfamily history. A stepfamily history is a step-by-step story of a stepfamily's beginning, development, and progress. These histories provide immeasurable benefits for stepfamilies. These benefits include:

- a written version of your experiences and journey into stepfamily success;

- an opportunity to create a written history of your life and the experiences and special moments that make your stepfamily unique;

- recorded memories for your stepchild;

- bragging rights at the stepfamily support group meeting!

Chapter 1

How Does Your
Stepfamily Measure Up?

Stepfamily. Even the word might give you goosebumps. It's the term "step"—as if to denote a secondary or "once removed" status. Traditional families with biologically related family members still seem to take precedence when we think of the word "family." Truth is, stepfamilies are beginning to outnumber traditional families, and on top of that, second marriages are breaking up faster than traditional or first-marriage families. Shocking? Yes. Unbelievable? Perhaps. At least that might be our emotional response. But we need to do more than just feel something about this reality. We need to do something to keep stepfamilies together—this is the task in front of us. But where do we begin? How can we keep our stepfamily healthy, happy, and functional and ensure its long life? Most of us said "'til death do us part." Now our challenge is to follow through on that promise to our spouses, ourselves, *and our* stepfamilies.

But is wanting your stepfamily to be successful and lasting enough? Sadly, no, but it's a great start. Committing to the success of your stepfamily is a huge first step toward the goal here. Each member of the stepfamily needs to commit to the work and dedication it will take to make your stepfamily work. So, let's create a great new start to your stepfamily. How? You are reading this book, and by doing so you have made the first move toward solidifying your future and the future of your family. Now let's act on that first step. Show your commitment by signing the following contract.

My Commitment to My Stepfamily's Success

I, _____ , will strive to understand and accept the challenges my stepfamily members and I will face in our efforts to create a successful and long-term stepfamily.

I will work hard to do my part toward this goal. I will respect my stepfamily members throughout this process, and I will try to understand any conflict and/or failures, learn to forgive my stepfamily members and myself, and move ahead supporting my stepfamily members with progress as the goal.

Stepparent: _____   Date: _____

Biological parent: _____   Date: _____

Stepchild: _____   Date: _____

Okay, great start. Keep this contract with your Stepfamily Plan. As you review your Stepfamily Plan in the future, reviewing this contract will remind you and your stepfamily members of your commitment to one another. Now, let's get to work.

Getting Started

As we discussed earlier, where do you begin? To use a cliché, you could "begin at the beginning," but for a stepfamily, the beginning may be at very different starting points given the unique circumstances that bring a stepfamily together. Why? Although the numbers of stepfamilies is large and on the rise, the differences between stepfamilies may outweigh the similarities. This is an interesting phenomenon, and frankly, can be a source of strength. How? What makes your stepfamily different may be a strength for its survival. For example, if your stepfamily differs because your relationship with your stepchild has been good from the start, that can strengthen the success of your stepfamily.

Conversely, these are also the differences that make it difficult to develop one single plan or strategy to help stepfamilies survive. So, the differences in your stepfamily can help strengthen your stepfamily but may or may not provide that same assistance to another stepfamily. This complicates things even more, and I think I know what you're thinking—that you cannot possibly create a stepfamily that capitalizes on your differences because it's those differences that often create the conflicts. You're right. Differences can *both* create strength and cause conflict. So sit up and take notice. You are about to become the smartest (and least confused) stepparent on the block.

Different Types of Stepfamilies

Why is it important to know the different types of stepfamilies? The biggest single reason is that this information will help you, as a stepparent, understand that other stepparents share in your journey but also to help you identify specific differences that may be strengths in your stepfamily. By understanding the similarities and the differences, you will learn to capitalize on those strengths to help build success in your stepfamily. We will also discuss parenting styles by reviewing the parenting styles you and your spouse have as well as realistically considering how to create a new, more effective parenting style for your stepfamily.

Stepfamily Type 1

A stepfamily with two parents who both have biological children.

This has the benefit of joining together a big family with lots of love to go around. However, the situation also has the potential for significant conflict. Why? Each parent may utilize different parenting styles for their own children. Bringing these styles together may confuse the children, particularly if the stepparent begins to engage in disciplining the children and the stepchildren are unfamiliar with the style used. This factor alone creates a lot of the conflict in stepfamilies, and if the disparity is not resolved, it can lead to problems in the stepfamily for the long term.

Consider whether your stepfamily situation is similar to Jon and Lizbeth's.

Case History: Jon and Lizbeth

Jon and Lizbeth had been struggling with how to parent their four children for the first four years of their marriage. After much trial and error, the conflicts that arose had taken a toll on the marriage. Jon and Lizbeth were exhausted and blaming each other for the failed parenting attempts. But what was the real problem? It wasn't that Jon and Lizbeth didn't love each other—they did. They were still both very committed to making the stepfamily work but their work was tiring and they were unable to see a way out.

Jon and Lizbeth examined their parenting by going back to the beginning, when they were first married. Each parent had two children and Jon and Lizbeth parented quite differently. Jon's kids were used to "getting their way on everything," as Lizbeth described it. Lizbeth was much more strict with rules and routines with her kids. This quickly became a problem once Jon and Lizbeth were married. In pinpointing the time frame of when the problem began, Jon and Lizbeth were able to understand that the first problem was that they did not plan ahead for parenting their four children together. The kids quickly picked up on the differences and took advantage of them. Jon's kids knew they had it easy with their dad, and this infuriated Lizbeth's kids because they didn't understand why they had to follow the rules and Jon's kids didn't.

After realizing that they needed to sit down and plan a new parenting style, Jon and Lizbeth listed the positives and the downsides of each of their parenting styles. Rather than focusing on the negative, Jon and Lizbeth took the positives out of each style and modified these into a new parenting style for their stepfamily. Once they were able to celebrate the positives, they also knew it was important to look at the differences to avoid future conflict by either parent slipping back into the former way of parenting. By doing this exercise, Jon and Lizbeth learned a great deal about themselves and their children's reactions and behaviors. They learned also how to be team members in managing a project for their stepfamily.

If your stepfamily situation is similar to this, do this exercise to get specific about the problem in your stepfamily.

Exercise: Your Parenting Style, Type 1

Bioparent: Briefly describe your parenting style.

Authoritative _____   Nurturing _____

Trying to be a Friend _____   Other _____

Stepparent: Briefly describe your parenting style.

Authoritative _____   Nurturing _____

Trying to be a Friend _____   Other _____

Build on your strengths. Identify the similarities between the two parenting styles in your stepfamily.

1. We both (circle all that apply):

    Offer encouragement   Offer choices

    Expect it to be our way   Expect respect and obedience

    Add your own: _____

2. Our biochildren respond to our parenting styles:

    Similarly   Very differently   Exactly the same

From this exercise you will begin to understand the basic similarities between you and your spouse's parenting styles. This is important because it gives you a starting point to build toward assimilating and creating a parenting style that may work for all of the children.

Now, let's look at the differences in your parenting styles. What is the single biggest difference that you see in the two parenting styles in your stepfamily? Circle all that apply?

- I/my spouse expect(s) too much from the kids.

- I/my spouse give(s) the children too many material things.

- I/my spouse parent(s) by a lot of guilt from the divorce.

- I/my spouse let(s) the kids make too many decisions.

- I/my spouse give(s) the kids too many choices.

Add your own. I/My spouse _____ .

Prioritize the issues. Which is the most important issue and needs to be worked on first? Make a priority list and give each priority a timeline.

#1 Issue _____

This will be completed by: _____

Okay, now you have your similarities and differences in front of you. By seeing them clearly, you can visualize where the parenting styles work effectively, and where the styles may break down.

Here is your opportunity to create a new parenting style by merging the two existing styles and adding new features. Below are some choices for you to consider adding to your parenting style.

What type of parenting style would work best for your stepfamily?

_____ More understanding   _____ More nurturing

_____ Less discipline   _____ More discipline

_____ Less angry tones   _____ More acceptance

_____ Stricter rules   _____ Less strict rules

_____ More choices for the children   _____ Fewer choices

_____ Defined boundaries

_____ More respect from the children

Now, create a new parenting style. The new parenting style for your stepfamily will be (choose all that fit):

_____ One that combines nurturing and discipline

_____ One that all the children are expected to follow

_____ More defined boundaries and more respect for parents

Now briefly write a description of your new parenting style.

_____

_____

_____

_____

_____

You can expect to see the results of your new parenting style in one to two months. The results you should see will be your stepchild responding more positively to you and a renewed strength in your marriage.

Jot down additional questions you want and need answers to right now. Remember, you can always contact me if you need help finding the answer.

Stepfamily Type 2

> # A stepfamily that has one bioparent and one adult without children.

Case History: Sara and Mason

Mason and Sara have a lovely family. He has children. She doesn't. More conflict arises from this type of stepfamily than any of the other situations. Why? If one adult has not had children before, the adjustment for the stepparent is considerable. Not having the parenting skills from having their own children may be problematic enough, but adding that to experimenting with parenting approaches with the stepchildren can lead to disaster. The relationship between the stepparent and stepchild can be harmed, and the marriage can be adversely affected also. Why? Because the bioparent may resent the stepparent's lack of parenting knowledge and unintentional efforts that may confuse the children. The stepparent wants so much to belong to this family and feels that participating in the parenting will cement their role in the stepfamily. However, if the stepchild is resistive to the stepparent's efforts, the problems begin and oftentimes escalate without resolution or getting to the heart of the conflict.

If your stepfamily is similar to this example, do this exercise.

Exercise: Your Parenting Style, Type 2

What concerns you about your parenting? Circle all that apply.

1. Your stepchild isn't listening to you.

2. Your stepchild is doing the opposite of what you have asked.

3. The bioparent is not supportive of your parenting.

It is important that you be specific on this and pinpoint the exact concerns. You need to know the exact problem before you can begin to solve it.

My concerns about my parenting are: _____

_____

_____

Rate your comfort level with parenting.

Very comfortable   Nervous   Scared to death   Not willing to parent

1   2   3   4

If you've decided not to parent but you're *very comfortable*, is it working okay for you not to parent? If yes, great. If not, discuss with the bioparent where conflicts and/or failures might be occurring.

If you're *nervous*, determine why. Ask the bioparent for help, particularly by discussing how the bioparent's parenting style works and how effective it is with the children. Below, describe the good points and possibly any downsides of the current parenting style.

Examples of good points

- The bioparent is direct and doesn't waver

- The kids respect the bioparent

- The kids want to please the parent

_____

_____

_____

If you're *scared to death*, you have your work cut out for you. Talk with the bioparent. Discuss what concerns you about parenting.

- Talk about maybe you taking a back seat until your comfort level is higher.

- Or discuss your options for leaving the parenting up to the bioparent.

If you are *unwilling to parent*, that is a normal reaction. However, discuss this with the bioparent, because your spouse may want you to help parent the children, and you do have a responsibility to your spouse on this.

Work out a plan of how you will approach this. Before you approach your partner to discuss this option, consider the following questions:

- Is your spouse okay with doing all of the parenting?

- What happens if you feel left out (because parenting is a huge part of a stepfamily)?

- What will you do if you begin to feel left out?

- If you choose not to parent, will the stepchildren view you as ineffective?

- If so, will this bother you?

List other questions you have and need answers to.

1. _____

2. _____

What type of parenting style would work best for you?

_____ More understanding _____ More nurturing

_____ Less discipline _____ More discipline

_____ Less angry tones _____ More acceptance

_____ Stricter rules _____ Less strict rules

_____ More choices for the children _____ Fewer choices

_____ Defined boundaries

_____ More respect from the children

Now, create a new parenting style. The new parenting style for your stepfamily will be (choose all that fit):

_____ One that combines nurturing and discipline

_____ One that all the children are expected to follow

_____ More defined boundaries and more respect for parents

Now briefly write a description of your new parenting style.

_____

_____

_____

_____

_____

Stepfamily Type #3

A stepfamily where a stepchild's other bioparent is absent either by death, abandonment, or her reason.

Case History: Raymond and Sidney

This is a difficult foundation for a stepfamily beginning. Why? Because normal development of a stepfamily brings conflicts and challenges and this stepfamily is challenged additionally with dealing with the emotions of loss. Can a stepfamily be successful with these added challenges? Absolutely, but a solid commitment and clearly set goals will be essential toward achieving the success you and your stepfamily so deserve.

Sidney and Raymond married about a year after Raymond's ex-wife died unexpectedly. Raymond has two children from this marriage, a teenage boy and girl. Sidney also has children, but her ex-spouse is still involved in the children's lives. The differences in the circumstances of the biological parents alone is an issue that needs to be discussed and treated sensitively prior to any stepfamily forming. Why? Because the children will be merging into a stepfamily for very different reasons, and those reasons may affect their emotional state about the stepfamily.

Also, Raymond will experience very different kinds and intensities of emotions about how his children will be treated by Sidney. This is because he's also still suffering under added emotional distress as a result of his previous wife dying. A divorce creates a certain set of emotions; the death of a spouse (even an ex-spouse) creates quite another set of emotions. This must be recognized and acknowledged by the adults involved prior to forming their stepfamily.

If your stepfamily is in this situation, complete this exercise.

Exercise: Your Parenting Style, Type 3

No matter what the reason is for an absent parent, this is a loss that your spouse and your stepchildren feel. This loss needs to be acknowledged and explored. Ask yourself these questions:

_____ Do you talk about the absent parent?

_____ Are the kids having a hard time with the loss?

_____ Is your spouse angry about the loss?

_____ Are you walking on eggshells about it?

Work out a plan of how to approach this.

1. Your spouse and stepchild need to understand that they've suffered a loss and it's okay to talk about it. Perhaps you have suffered a loss also.

2. A variety of emotions may emerge when this is acknowledged by your stepfamily members. The following suggestions may help your stepfamily but please discuss with your spouse:

    a. Seek a support group

    b. Seek professional counseling

    c. Encourage your spouse and stepchild to release emotions in their own way and at their own pace. Encourage your stepchild to write a letter to the person who is gone

    d. Keep a daily journal of thoughts and feelings associated with the loss expressed

    e. Explore any feelings of guilt or blame surrounding the loss

    f. The goal is for acceptance so the stepfamily can move ahead together

    g. It is especially important that the stepchild can move ahead because this will help the progress of your stepchild

3. Keep the memory alive of the parent who is absent. That parent is still part of your spouse and stepchild's lives.

4. The spouse must be sure to recognize the stepparent as a separate individual and not consistently compare the stepparent with their former spouse.

5. The stepparent must help their new spouse in this process—be supportive.

List questions you need answers to right now.

1. _____

2. _____

What type of parenting style would work best for your stepfamily?

_____ More understanding   _____ More nurturing

_____ Less discipline   _____ More discipline

_____ Less angry tones   _____ More acceptance

_____ Stricter rules   _____ Less strict rules

_____ More choices for the children   _____ Fewer choices

_____ Defined boundaries

_____ More respect from the children

Now, create a new parenting style. The new parenting style for your stepfamily will be (choose all that fit):

_____ One that combines nurturing and discipline

_____ One that all the children are expected to follow

_____ More defined boundaries and more respect for parents

Now briefly write a description of your new parenting style.

_____

_____

_____

_____

Stepfamily Type #4

> # A stepfamily where the ex-spouse is an active participant in the raising of the children.

Case History: Ken and Crystal

At the outset, having an additional adult to parent the children appears to be a healthy and desirable trait for biological parents divorcing and remarrying. Why? Having an additional parent allows the other parents a break, which helps the parents forming a stepfamily to have time to develop and maintain their new marriage. There are also conflicts that can occur in this type of stepfamily. The conflicts in this type center around the boundaries between the parents that used to be married in terms of just how involved the other parent will be in the new stepfamily's life. The Stepfamily Plan in this book focuses a great deal on the need for a parenting team, which is a necessity for consistent parenting of children involved in stepfamilies. However, the issue of boundaries with each parent is critical to the success of not only the Stepfamily Plan but the stepfamily itself. Why? Because the ex-spouse is not allowed to overstep the boundaries set up by the biological parent and the stepparent. If boundaries are not set for the ex-spouse, the potential exists for the ex-spouse to be intrusive and interfering in the newly formed stepfamily. This type of situation can lead to the deterioration of the stepfamily.

Crystal and Ken are happily married. There's only one problem—Crystal's ex-husband seems to think that he's still married to Crystal, at least as far as the parenting of the children is concerned. This is where it gets a little confusing because we want the bioparent to remain involved in the children's lives, right? Yes. But if the bioparent is overly involved, the situation can get a bit sticky. For example, take a situation where the biological mother of the children insists on making rules for the children not only at her house, but she also insists that the children follow these same rules at their father's house. The father and stepparent may or may not agree with the mother's rules and may not want to include the mother's rules. What do you do?

If this is similar to your stepfamily, try this exercise.

Exercise: Your Parenting Style, Type 4

Do all parents currently work together to parent?   Yes/No

Is the parenting done consistently now from house to house? Yes/No

Are boundaries clearly in place for all parents?   Yes/No

Does the ex-spouse understand what is acceptable
and what is not?   Yes/No

If you answered "No" to any of the above questions, you are at the stage in your stepfamily where you need to create your parenting plan. The parenting plan will provide you:

1. A consistent and guaranteed plan for the parenting of the stepchildren

2. Consistent guidelines for each parent for parental involvement and limitations

3. A method to merge your parenting styles for greater parenting consistency

What is the first step you need to take toward building a parenting plan? Call a family meeting with the ex-spouses and clearly outline this by stating your intentions for the parenting plan. Use this book as your focal point of the family meeting. Each parent should have a copy to follow to make notes and complete the exercises provided.

What type of parenting style would work best for your stepfamily?

_____ More understanding _____ More nurturing

_____ Less discipline _____ More discipline

_____ Less angry tones _____ More acceptance

_____ Stricter rules _____ Less strict rules

_____ More choices for the children _____ Fewer choices

_____ Defined boundaries

_____ More respect from the children

Now, create a new parenting style. The new parenting style for your stepfamily will be (choose all that fit):

____ One that combines nurturing and discipline

____ One that all the children are expected to follow

____ More defined boundaries and more respect for parents

Now briefly write a description of your new parenting style.

_____

_____

_____

_____

_____

Stepfamily Type 5

A stepfamily where the ex-spouse chooses not to participate in raising the kids.

Case History: Quinton and Maris

Maris and Quinton are raising Maris' children together without the help of the children's father. To be honest, this situation is pretty close to the ideal stepfamily! No bothersome ex-spouse. No problems with visitation schedules. No problems with parenting consistency from home to home. No problem, right? Sadly, no. Even though this may seem like the ideal situation, there are still conflicts that will occur. A lot of conflict may erupt because the burden of the parenting lies with Maris and Quinton alone. They rarely get a break. The consistency is there for the children, but they miss their other parent and struggle with why their other parent is not involved with their lives. Responsibility for the parenting becomes a burden for Maris and Quinton, and they are at a loss to explain the father's absence to their children because the ex-spouse refuses to discuss this with the kids.

If your stepfamily is similar, try this.

Exercise: Your Parenting Style, Type 5

Describe the best thing about this situation in your stepfamily.

Bioparent _____

_____

Stepparent _____

_____

Describe the toughest issue in dealing with this absent other parent.

Bioparent _____

_____

Stepparent _____

_____

What would you want changed in this situation?

Bioparent _____

_____

Stepparent _____

_____

Do you think these changes are realistic?

    Bioparent ____ yes ____ no

    Stepparent ____ yes ____ no

If yes, then list what you are willing to do to help change this situation to make your stepfamily better: _____

_____

_____

If no, then move on. Don't dwell on something that cannot and will not be changed in your stepfamily. Understand this—it's vital to the success of your stepfamily.

List questions you need answers to right now.

1. _____

2. _____

What type of parenting style would work best for your stepfamily?

_____ More understanding   _____ More nurturing

_____ Less discipline   _____ More discipline

_____ Less angry tones   _____ More acceptance

_____ Stricter rules   _____ Less strict rules

_____ More choices for the children   _____ Fewer choices

_____ Defined boundaries

_____ More respect from the children

Now, create a new parenting style. The new parenting style for your stepfamily will be (choose all that fit):

_____ One that combines nurturing and discipline

_____ One that all the children are expected to follow

_____ More defined boundaries and more respect for parents

Now briefly write a description of your new parenting style.

_____

_____

_____

_____

_____

Stepfamily Type #6

A stepfamily where the ex-spouse is a reluctant parent only.

Case Study: Weston and Hillary

Having an additional parent only some of the time may seem ideal initially; however, conflicts can occur and may be more significant from a reluctant or part-time parent looking in from the outside of your stepfamily. Why? A reluctant outside parent may offer a break at times for you, but may not be able to maintain the consistency in the parenting from house to house that is so needed with a stepfamily situation. A parent that looks in from the outside can be critical and judgmental of your parenting if they are involved only to a point because they will see only a portion of the whole picture of the parenting. A reluctant parent may also make demands that may seem unreasonable given their limited involvement with the children. Oftentimes, the full-time biological parent and stepparent begin to feel taken advantage of by the reluctant parent, and the breakdown in communication begins toward a deterioration in the parenting altogether.

Hillary and Weston felt their problems would significantly decrease due to Weston's ex-wife not wanting a lot of contact. In the beginning, this worked out fine, and there was little conflict because Hillary and Weston didn't often have to deal with another parent. However, they were concerned for the children's benefit. A reluctant bioparent in a stepfamily situation means minimal contact with the children.

Gradually conflicts did arise out of this situation. Although Hillary and Weston handled the bulk of the parenting, they soon realized that Weston's ex-spouse appeared highly critical of their parenting decisions. Hillary and Weston felt she was being unreasonable, given that they were doing the majority of the work with the kids. Weston's ex-wife seemed to take advantage of Weston and Hillary taking most of the responsibility. She would often not pick the kids up when she said she would, and she would consistently change the visitation schedules. When the children needed their mother at parent-teacher conferences or at dance recitals, the mother was inconsistent in attending. This unreliability caused emotional strain for the children, which in turn caused emotional turbulence in the stepfamily. It seemed that the mother was the source of much conflict but was not there to help fix it. The situation became complicated for Hillary and Weston, particularly because they could not rely on Weston's ex-spouse nor could the children, which caused emotional insecurities for the kids and instability for the stepfamily.

If you are dealing with this situation, let's examine it in this way.

Exercise: Parenting Style, Type 6

List the positive ways the other parent does help contribute. You might start with things like:

- It gives you and your spouse a break.

- The other parent is cooperative in making arrangements.

Add your own: _____

Now, list the problems as you see them.

1. The other parent "buys" the kids.

2. The other parent uses the kids to get to you and your spouse.

3. The stepchild is upset when his parent doesn't come through.

Add your own: _____

First, prioritize the problems, and tackle only the ones that you feel can truly be improved.

How do you begin to problem solve?

1. Understand the children's feelings about the level of their other parent's involvement.

2. Is this contact best for the children? If so, then the bioparent and stepparent need to create the "rules of involvement" for the other parent.

3. Your parenting team must establish consistency in the rules.

4. Who will discuss this with the ex-spouse? _____

5. Set a deadline for this to be accomplished: _____

List questions you have right now.

1. _____

2. _____

What type of parenting style would work best for your stepfamily?

_____ More understanding   _____ More nurturing

_____ Less discipline   _____ More discipline

_____ Less angry tones   _____ More acceptance

_____ Stricter rules   _____ Less strict rules

_____ More choices for the children   _____ Fewer choices

_____ Defined boundaries

_____ More respect from the children

Now, create a new parenting style. The new parenting style for your stepfamily will be (choose all that fit):

_____ One that combines nurturing and discipline

_____ One that all the children are expected to follow

_____ More defined boundaries and more respect for parents

Now briefly write a description of your new parenting style.

_____

_____

_____

_____

It is important that you understand the type of stepfamily you have before you actually create a stepfamily plan. This includes knowing the factors that brought you together in the first place, how you feel about one another, if you are comfortable in the role as stepparent, if you are comfortable with how you and your spouse parent. There is one additional point that is beneficial for you to think about, and that is what makes your stepfamily unique. The very thing that makes your stepfamily unique may become a strength for you in creating your stepfamily plan. We will discuss this in detail in a later chapter.

You're Different—and the Same

Different stepfamilies possess unique differences. However, these very same stepfamilies share similarities that allow the opportunity to develop a Stepfamily Plan that can be applied across the board in all of the different stepfamilies.

Let's start with the differences. First, there is the individual makeup of the personalities operating in each stepfamily. Stepfamilies consist of assertive stepparents and insecure, uncertain stepparents. Stepfamilies also consist of bioparents with these same characteristics. The personalities of stepchildren differ across each family type, ranging from cooperative to oppositional.

Another difference is how the stepfamilies came to be formed in the first place. Each set of adults met in different ways and under different circumstances. These circumstances bring a variety of issues to each stepfamily, such as acceptance by the extended family or visitation schedules that differ with each set of stepchildren.

Each adult may have a different parenting style. Each parenting style has a set of differences that need to be integrated in the parenting team rules of the game. Other differences include the stepparent's attitude toward the stepchildren or the stepparent's vision for the stepfamily. Often, a lot of the differences in stepfamilies center around the attitude of the stepfamily toward the core families they joined. The core families, which consisted of the bioparents and their children have a set of traditions and routines established long before the stepparent came on the scene. Each stepfamily differs in these traditions and routines, and each stepfamily may, in fact, deal differently with these sets of traditions and routines.

Now, let's look at the similarities in the same stepfamily types. But wait. Similarities? You just read about the *differences* in stepfamilies. There are similarities in these stepfamilies too? You bet. That's the beauty of a stepfamily. Although your stepfamily has differences from every other stepfamily out there (that also act as your strengths), your stepfamily also has similarities to every other stepfamily out there. It may seem strange, because when you experience conflict in your stepfamily, you often feel like you are the only stepparent in the world going through this. You may also feel that no one else could really understand what you are going through. The problem with these feelings is that, as a stepparent, you probably feel alienated when insecurity about the conflicts in your stepfamily come up, and instead of realizing that other stepparents are feeling and experiencing the very same problems, you may tend to struggle through the conflict on your own, groping your way to some kind of resolution. And sometimes that resolution simply doesn't come. You then probably begin to feel defeated, and if and when that happens, you begin the stepparent downward spiral dance of trying to juggle this problem by yourself. If you feel, as the stepparent, that you have to solve these problems alone, without the help of your spouse, it may just become too much. You may want to simply give up.

So stepparents of the world—unite! You are not alone. You have comrades out there who are struggling with the same issues. They may even have arrived at a problem-solving strategy that may work in your stepfamily. The best gift stepparents can give to each other is to *share* what has worked and we can do this by beginning to understand the similarities in our stepfamilies.

Similarities in stepfamilies include the challenges faced in combining families, experiencing similar conflicts, struggling with ones such as alienation, insanity and, often, ex-spouses. Stepfamilies share common bonds in areas other families do not, particularly living with someone else's children, learning how to discipline someone elses children, and dealing with emotions many people find intolerable such as rejection from stepchildren.

By now you should have a good idea of the complicated makeup of stepfamilies, including your stepfamily. At this point, you should also have an idea of the differences and similarities in your stepfamily as compared to other stepfamilies out there. How *does* your stepfamily compare?

Below is the first page of your Stepfamily Journal. One of the most important techniques in constructing a Stepfamily Plan (as we're about to do) is to build your Stepfamily History. What is the best way to do that? By creating a journal of your thoughts and activities, particularly as you journey through this book and complete the exercises, customizing experiences to your own stepfamily. I encourage you to record your stepfamily's history and experiences as you go through this book and build your plan. Creating a Stepfamily History allows you to be in your role as stepparent by taking initiative toward creating your own stepfamily with your stepfamily members, the most important people in your life.

One of the greatest benefits of this book is that by working through the exercises you are building your Stepfamily Plan. By building your Stepfamily Plan, you are creating your Stepfamily History. Each step of your Stepfamily History is created with your completed journal entry at the end of each chapter. You will record your memories and experiences in developing your stepfamily through this book, and your efforts will be rewarded in what is called your Stepfamily History. Many people long for a recorded history of their family. By working through this book, you are creating your Stepfamily History as a gift to you and your stepfamily for cherished memories and years to come. As a team you build your stepfamily, nurture it, transform it, and live it. And the first step is with your first journal page.

My Stepfamily Journal

After reading this chapter, take a few minutes and jot down how you are feeling about your stepfamily right now. Have you identified what type of stepfamily you are in or is your stepfamily type unique? If so, write a few lines to describe exactly what your stepfamily type is. Then write down areas in your stepfamily that need improvement right now. Make a list of what you can do right now to start those improvements, such as:

1. Continue to read this book for more information on what to expect in my stepfamily development

Congratulations. You have done a wonderful job toward helping develop a healthy and positive stepfamily. Information in this chapter helped you identify what type of stepfamily you are living in. Knowing this will help you understand what problems or sensitive areas you may need to look for and be working on in your stepfamily. This will help you focus your energy on the specific problem areas and not try to tackle all conflicts and problems at once. Your goal is to develop a successful stepfamily. You start by knowing your beginnings. Now let's dive into the next area that we need to know and understand completely before we begin building our Stepfamily Plan—knowing the stepparenting myths and realities to help sort out the realities of stepfamily life and present a clear and accurate picture of what you can expect from your journey.

Chapter 2

Stepparenting Myths
and Realities

A discussion of stepfamilies would not be complete without a look at certain myths and realities of stepparenting. Now that you know some of the differences and similarities between stepfamilies, let's try to dispel some of the myths you may have heard about stepparenting.

In working with stepfamilies over the years, I have seen how difficult it can be for new stepparents to see past the myths they have brought with them into their stepfamilies. Although it's difficult to change your perceptions, it can be done. You will have a chance in this section to explore any myths that you may have come with into your stepparenting role and have the opportunity to dispel them so your outlook and energy into your role as stepparent can become more proactive.

Many myths about stepparenting have crossed the minds of stepparents everywhere. These myths serve no particular purpose other than to give an inaccurate first impression. Therefore it's important to talk about the myths that exist about stepparenting, and beyond that, to help you identify any myths or inaccuracies that have influenced your role as stepparent. In my work with stepparents, I have identified the following list of working myths about stepparenting.

Myth 1: The Stepparent Will Always Be Included

> # Does this myth apply to you?
> ____ Yes   ____ No

Think back to when you first entered your role as stepparent. If you were included in all family activities, congratulations. Your stepfamily would be exceptional in that respect, and I would assert that you were given a "gift" by your stepfamily. The reality of most stepfamilies is that the stepparent will *not* be included in all of activities in the family. Why? Because the core family had preestablished activities that they did together, and your spouse and his or her children are going to continue with some of those activities. An example would be a discussion between your spouse and his or her children about their college funds. (Later on in this book, I'll expand on this example in the section devoted to planning your ideal family. You'll learn which topics will require discussion *prior* to the marriage.) As far as myths are concerned, however, it's important to start off on the right foot. You will be acting proactively in your role by being prepared for this exclusion from certain activities. If you enter into your stepfamily expecting that you will be included in all activities, then the first time you discover you're not included, feelings of rejection and of being an outsider emerge. So do yourself a favor. Accept the fact that you probably won't be included in each and every activity that your stepfamily members are involved in.

If you know ahead of time that you will not be included in certain activities and you know what those activities are, you have saved yourself a significant amount of stress by being prepared for this "planned rejection." You will also have saved your stepfamily from significant conflict that may have relived itself over and over again, each time this activity came up. By avoiding this stepfamily frustration, you single-handedly have helped your stepfamily take a step toward greater progress. So understand that you will not be included in some family activities that will continue in your new stepfamily, and accept it. Plan for rejection and don't let rejection control you.

So, does this myth apply to you? Did you feel that you would be included in all activities in your stepfamily? If so, list one thing you can do to "fix" this in your stepfamily, and resolve to work on it:

_____

_____

Myth 2: The Ex-Spouse Is Gone

> # Does this myth apply to you?
> ____ Yes ____ No

Okay, who believed the ex-spouse would be out of your new spouse's life? Go ahead. Be honest. This is a safe place to share your innermost thoughts and feelings. At some point, I actually thought this about my stepfamily. Why? It's part of the fantasy world stepparents sometimes create for themselves. You may have created one also when you first fell in love with a person who is also a biological parent. By clinging to this myth, you avoid facing the fact that the ex-spouse actually *will* be involved with your spouse and *should* be in order to effectively parent their children through and after divorce. Even a deceased ex-spouse or one who abandoned the family is still a presence. What is your role in this? Your job is to understand that your spouse's ex will be involved, both in the children's lives and in your spouse's. The level of this involvement will depend upon the unique circumstances of your step-family. Your job is to accept the amount of time the ex-spouse will be involved. Stepparents are often disappointed to find just how much the ex-spouse actually is still involved with the new stepfamily. I call this "planned disappointment." Why? Part of being proactive in your stepfamily is to plan ahead, right? So why not plan ahead for disappointment? For example, if you know that the ex-spouse will be involved in your new stepfamily but still are surprised when it's longer and deeper than you thought, you may still feel disappointment. Knowing in advance that this may happen can protect you from serious, unexpected disappointment that may negatively affect you and your stepfamily. So, be the most progressive stepparent on the block and plan for disappointment. You will benefit from this in the long run.

Exercise: How to Plan Ahead for Disappointment

What's the best way to handle planned disappointment? Prepare for it ahead of time. Let's practice preparing for disappointment by making a list now of issues (including this one) that you see in your stepfamily where you may feel disappointment.

1. I have felt disappointment when my spouse _____

_____

_____

_____

2. I have felt disappointment when my stepchild _____

_____

_____

_____

3. My stepfamily has felt disappointment when I _____

_____

_____

_____

In stepfamilies, it's helpful to prepare for disappointment ahead of time. It allows each of you to control this emotion and not allow it to control you.

So dispelling the myth is to be prepared for disappointment. This is sounding like loads of fun so far. But seriously, if we do plan ahead for things that may take us off balance, we can reduce the stress they cause, thereby reducing the frustration and anger that are a given in a stepparent's life. And what is the reality here? The reality is that the ex-spouse will be in your new spouse's life. So surprise your new spouse by understanding this up front and not getting angry about it. If you handle it in this way, you will be cementing your stepfamily's future as well as creating a healthy new you for your stepfamily to enjoy.

Take a minute to evaluate. Does this myth now apply to you? If so, what one thing can you do to fix this in your stepfamily and work to resolve it? _____

_____

_____

_____

Myth 3: The Stepparent Isn't in Competition with the Ex

Does this myth apply to you?
____ Yes ____ No

Yes, you read that correctly. You're probably thinking that you don't compete with the ex-spouse, and if you don't, that's great. But if you do, you would not be the first stepparent to feel this way. You're not alone. Actually, most stepparents do feel in competition with their spouse's ex. It's natural for you to feel in competition with a person your new spouse had a life with previously. The key to your success with this challenge is to not get wrapped up in jealousy or the suspicion that your spouse still has feelings for their ex-spouse. Let's clear that up right now. Your spouse *does* have feelings for their ex-spouse. What kind of feelings depends upon your spouse and the circumstances of their divorce. Remember, that happened before you, so if your opinion about that isn't particularly pleasant, then it may not be welcome. Generally, no matter what the circumstances are with the ex, the reality is that you will compete in some ways with the ex-spouse. It's okay to admit that. The real challenge is for you to confront it, accept it, and overcome it. Let's evaluate this. Does this myth apply to you? If so, what one thing can you do to fix this in your stepfamily and work to resolve it? _____

_____

_____

_____

Myth 4: A Stepparent Doesn't Compete with their Stepchild

> ## Does this myth apply to you?
> ____ Yes ____ No

Most stepparents would understandably rather not admit to this one. Why? Because you are an adult and as an adult, how on earth could you possibly compete with a child, particularly a stepchild? It's not adult-like. That's right, it's not "adult-like." But the reality is that many stepparents *do* compete with their stepchild, and not acknowledging it causes more conflict in your stepfamily. Why? A stepparent will often try to mask these feelings with some other problem because it's painful to admit to them. Your first reaction probably would be to deny that you compete with your stepchild. However, what you need to do is admit it, identify the feelings that fact brings, and by acknowledging how you feel, you can then work to reconcile the situation. If you can admit the problem, then you can solve it.

Solving this one is big, but you can do it. Getting past this can help your stepfamily plan much better for the future with this concern out of the way. So let's evaluate. Does this myth apply to you? If so, what one thing can you do to fix this in your stepfamily? _____

_____

_____

_____

Myth 5: You Won't Feel Undervalued by Your Stepchild

> ## Does this myth apply to you?
> ____ Yes ____ No

Here's a news flash. You *will* feel undervalued by your stepchild in spite of your valiant efforts to become their parent, friend, mentor, or whatever role you wanted to create with your stepchild. If that is disappointing to you (and here's an opportunity to plan disappointment), believe it or not, that is a step in the right direction. Why? Because it means that you care about your stepchild, and that's the beginning of a beautiful relationship. All stepparents tend to feel undervalued by their stepchild. Why? It goes back to our expectations as stepparents. We tend to expect a lot from our stepchild, and we usually expect our stepchild to appreciate us immediately. In the majority of stepfamilies, this will not happen. If we've expected it and it doesn't happen, we then feel rejected and let down by our stepchild. These feelings lead to us feeling that our role in the stepfamily is not valuable, which affects not only how we perform as stepparents but also every member of our stepfamily. You need to be aware of these repercussions and be honest with yourself about your feelings and expectations. Do you feel undervalued by *your* stepchild?

But the real question is, how can we avoid feeling undervalued by our stepchildren? The best prevention for this would be to expect that it may happen to you. And you can do this by knowing that your stepchild needs time to get to know you. They will always feel their bioparents are more significant to them. That's normal. It does not mean that you are any less valuable in the stepfamily. Understand this. So, let's evaluate. Does this myth now apply to you? If so, what one thing can you do to fix this in your stepfamily and work toward resolving it?

_____

_____

_____

Myth 6: The Stepparent Will Control Decisions That Affect the Stepchild

> ## Does this myth apply to you?
> ____ Yes   ____ No

When you become a stepparent, something strange happens. A transformation occurs where you begin to feel that you will play an instrumental role in your stepfamily as an authority figure and, if all goes well, parent. Great—so what's the problem? The problem comes in when we make an assumption that this will automatically occur when we sign on with the stepfamily. The reality is, however, that you will not start out with control over the decision making that affects your stepchild, and you may never have it. Why? It's a huge expectation, and it's unrealistic. You are not the bioparent. That title allows you privileges and rewards that a stepparent must earn, if you are fortunate enough to ever be a parent to your stepchild. Being able to exercise control over decision making that affects your stepchild is a gift. If your spouse feels you are entitled to that gift, you will be fortunate indeed.

But what if that doesn't happen? You may become disappointed, confused, feel rejected, and perhaps begin to withdraw from your stepfamily because you feel like an outcast or an insignificant member. Why? Because you may feel it's your right as a stepparent to be involved in the decision making for your stepchild. After all, you are part of the stepfamily, part of the team that manages this stepfamily. Without this granted authority, you may feel less important and perhaps even untrustworthy. These feelings can get out of control, so it's important to know ahead of time how this myth can affect you. Let's reevaluate. If you feel this myth applies to you, what one thing can you do to help your stepfamily and resolve this myth? _____

_____

_____

_____

Myth 7: The Stepparent Will Always Know Their Status

Does this myth apply to you?
____ Yes ____ No

As a stepparent, you want to know where you stand with your new spouse and with your stepchild. This is important to your security in the stepfamily. The reality of this situation, however, is that you won't always know where you stand in the pecking order in your stepfamily. Why? Because your role can change from day to day and even from situation to situation. For example, one day you may be sure of your position in the stepfamily as parent and co-captain of the parenting team. The next day, a new situation may occur where your spouse feels that only they should handle this particular issue with their child. Suddenly you feel you have lost ground, but you're not sure how or why or what to do about it. This is often one of the most frustrating and difficult situations for the stepparent. Stepparents want a degree of control over their situation just as the bioparent does. The difference is that stepparents aren't always in a position to determine what will happen or how things will go.

For example, if you expect that you will be an equal coparent and authority figure, only to discover that your spouse doesn't see you this way, then that old feeling of rejection and insecurity may return to you. Or if your spouse wants you to coparent and be an authority figure to your stepchildren, but you feel uncomfortable with this, you may also feel unsure about where you stand. What is the best way for stepparents to be proactive about their role and status? Be flexible. Be prepared for changes in your role. Let's reevaluate and try to understand if you can do this. Does this myth apply to you? If so, what one thing can you do to help dispel this myth and help you handle this changing role in your stepfamily? _____

_____

_____

Myth 8: You Won't Have to Struggle with This Marriage

Does this myth apply to you?
_____ Yes _____ No

Whether this marriage is your second, third, or beyond, who *doesn't* struggle with making a marriage work? As a stepparent, not only do you have work to do in bonding with your stepchild, but you have the added pressure of making your marriage a success. Where do you find the energy for all of this? Within you, that's where. You make your stepfamily and marriage a priority in your life. It is more important than work. It is more important than shopping. It is more important than *anything else*. Think of your stepfamily first, before you make decisions about things. Is this best for your stepfamily? Do not be selfish. You are no longer a single unit looking only at what is best for you as an individual person.

Try this. Put your stepfamily's needs before your own. Put your marriage's needs before your own. This is a sacrifice that will pay off in a grand reward of achieving a successful marriage and stepfamily. What one thing can you do for the health of your marriage today? _____

_____

_____

_____

Myth 9: You Won't Feel Alienated

Does this myth apply to you?
____ Yes ____ No

Okay, let's be realistic about this one. As a stepparent, you will feel alienated at one time or another in your stepfamily life, by any number of people in your immediate stepfamily or in the extended families. Why? Partly because of the expectations we have about our role in this new stepfamily and partly because of the nature of the stepfamily itself. Stepparents are not included in all family matters, as we have discussed earlier. Sometimes extended family members verbally exclude us. This does happen. My hope is that it will not happen in your stepfamily. However, if you underestimate this or disregard it, you may feel increased alienation.

As a stepparent, you can prevent alienation or stop it from happening to you. How? By being proactive and taking charge of this situation. The key question is, what can *you do* to avoid feeling alienated in your stepfamily? The following are several suggestions for you to start considering today:

- Develop a bond with your stepchild

- Develop a relationship with extended family members

- Don't isolate yourself

- Stay positive and hopeful about the stepfamily's future

- Do your part to help your stepfamily be successful

Does this myth apply to you? If so, what can you do to ensure that you will not feel alienated in your stepfamily?

_____

_____

_____

Myth 10: You Will Be Accepted by the Extended Family Immediately

Does this myth apply to you?
_____ Yes _____ No

The answer is probably not. Hey, give them a break. They don't know you, but they do know the history of the family core prior to your entrance into this stepfamily. There may be feelings of uncertainty about you or uncomfortable feelings about the original family breaking up. Whatever the reason, it will take time for the extended family to accept you. What's your job? Allow the extended family members the time they need to get to know you. You've got the time. You've got the rest of your life to become an accepted and strong member of your stepfamily. Relax and let them get to know you slowly. Let them get to know the person who will play a big part in making this newly created stepfamily work. It's well worth the time and energy spent.

Does this myth apply to you? If so, what is one thing you can do to help your extended family accept you? _____

_____

_____

_____

Myth 11: You Will Be Number One

Does this myth apply to you?
____ Yes ____ No

This would be great, wouldn't it? But the reality of the stepfamily is that you will not be number one in your spouse's life. Why? Because your spouse has children, plain and simple. Your stepchild will come first because they need parenting and parenting is a full-time job for not only your spouse, but for you and any ex-spouse involved. You can be number one in your spouse's life after the kids leave for college. Let your stepchildren have this time with their bioparents. You owe this to your spouse and to your stepfamily. Give of yourself, and you will receive greater rewards in the long run.

What are the rewards of being secondary in your spouse's life?

1. You will increase the intimacy and strength of your marriage.

2. Your spouse may not be spending all of their time alone with you, but they will be thinking of you a lot more.

3. You will be assured that you did the right thing for your spouse and for your stepfamily.

4. You are loved.

Exercise: Exploring Your *Myths*

This is your chance to dispel those myths that you have come into your role with. Add the myths of your own that you believed about this role:

_____

_____

_____

What can you do to change this?

_____

_____

_____

Many myths are generated from this difficult job we call stepparenting. Why? Because the role is a desirable one, but the perception about being a stepparent and the actual role are quite different. You won't discover that until you actually become a stepparent. However, the beauty of being a stepparent is that you *can* let go of the harmful myths and perceptions and play a key role in building a strong, healthy stepfamily. It's time that stepparents take a more realistic and proactive role in their stepfamilies. In your stepfamily, that begins with you and *The Stepparent's Survival Guide.*

My Stepfamily Journal

Chapter 3

Stepparent Beliefs: Preconceived Ideas That Can and Will Affect Your Stepfamily

In the last chapter we discussed general myths that many stepparents have about life in a stepfamily. In this chapter, we dig deeper into how you, as an individual, carry specific beliefs and preconceived ideas you may not even be aware of into your new role as stepparent. Just as in a new job or any new situation that may be unfamiliar, you will have preconceived ideas about how your stepfamily will look and what it will be like to be a member of the family. Preconceived ideas can be helpful, but these same ideas can also provide negative affects on relationships. Preconceived ideas usually come from something we've learned either through our own mistakes or hearing it from others. Beliefs about future marriages and becoming a stepparent are issues that you need to explore for your role as stepparent. Why is this important? Because beliefs can affect how you will perform in a stepfamily and in your role as stepparent. Let's take a look at your beliefs and learn how they can affect you and your stepfamily.

First we need to discuss the power of beliefs. What is this power about? Well, beliefs are those ideas that have influenced our perception of events or people prior to us actually engaging in that event or meeting that person. Think about the job that you hold. The thoughts that you had about this job prior to starting it would fall under the category of preconceived ideas. What will the work be like? Will I like it? What will my office be like? How well will I work with my supervisor? All of these questions and thoughts are conceptualized and even partially "answered" prior to you actually starting that job. For example, you may have particular beliefs about the organization you're about to work for. These beliefs may be from talking to someone who works there or through your first impressions at the interview. Can these preconceived ideas affect your performance on the job? The answer is yes. Any ideas or thoughts that you have prior to engaging in an act can and will affect your performance and even how you like the job. Why? Because these ideas strongly influence how we will feel about the job. This influence is powerful enough to taint how we feel about a certain job or position.

This scenario can also occur prior to being a stepparent. For example, if we hear only negatives about being a stepparent, we will be negatively influenced into believing that being a stepparent is not a pleasant and enjoyable role but rather a disappointing and undesirable one. So how do these beliefs begin and what can we do to change them if they lead us into a negative mind-set?

In order to understand this concept more clearly, let's look at examples of beliefs that you may have had or have now about being a stepparent. Below is a list of beliefs that stepparents have discussed with me in my practice about how they felt prior to entering their role as stepparent:

- The stepparent has to adapt to their spouse's routines and traditions

- The stepparent will *always* be the outsider

- The stepparent should try to please the stepchild and be a friend

- The stepparent wants to be first but has no idea how to accomplish this

- The stepparent's spouse will see how unfair it is to side with the stepchild all of the time

- The stepparent's spouse will do everything to make the stepfamily work

Belief 1: The Stepparent Must Adapt

Let's look at each example of beliefs about stepparenting and explain just how these ideas can influence your performance as a stepparent. First, let's explore the idea of having to adapt to your spouse's routines. This is a very common belief that stepparents bring into their role as stepparent. You will want to try and accommodate your new spouse and your stepchild as much as possible. As a result, you feel that one way of doing this will be for you to adjust to your new environment which already consists of established family routines and traditions. You will not want to make waves and to try and "fit in" as much as possible. This is a wonderful idea and a selfless act of tolerance toward your step-family. However, after you have done this for some time, you begin to feel that you are doing all of the work. You may begin to wonder, "What adjustments are my spouse and stepchild making here?" This is a common situation with stepparents. Why? The stepparent is generally considered the newcomer, and in that role, the stepparent is expected to adjust to the family already in place. Initially, wanting to cooperate and do what you can to help things go smoothly, you make the adjustments. After some time this may feel like work, and becoming tired, you may begin to question what the other members in your stepfamily are doing to help things go smoothly.

It's not wrong for you to want to adjust to the established routines, but after a while, you may begin to feel a dissatisfaction in your role as stepparent. Feeling this way can contribute to feelings of alienation. So how do we reduce or even try to eliminate these feelings? By being proactive as a stepparent and not falling into the power of this belief of you doing the adjusting to the routines in your stepfamily. Your particular stepfamily can be different. You can control your performance. One of the best ways to accomplish this is by recognizing beliefs that you have about your role as stepparent and proactively changing and modifying those ideas now, before you find yourself in a situation that is uncomfortable for you. Identify and recognize beliefs that may be influencing how you are functioning in your stepfamily. This is key to recognizing the need to change your belief system about your role and what you perceive to be expected of you by your stepfamily members.

Why would a stepparent feel this way? There are lots of reasons, actually. You'll want your stepfamily members to like you, so you will try everything you can do to make sure this happens. You won't want to rock the boat and one of the best ways to not rock anything is to be the one to make the adjustments. You may feel that having only one person in the stepfamily making the adjustments will make it easier on everybody else. And in general this is absolutely true.

So you come into your stepfamily and feel that you will be able to adjust to their routines and traditions without difficulty. On the outside, this appears to be an incredibly generous gesture on your part, and initially your stepfamily members may feel appreciative. On all accounts, it *is* incredibly generous on your part. Unconsciously, you may feel that if you make all of the adjustments, then your stepfamily members will like you and your stepfamily will move along more smoothly. But what happens if it doesn't work out this way? That's when the belief becomes a liability to your stepfamily. Something that starts out so positively and well meaning can turn into a problematic situation for you and your stepfamily. Why? Because your stepfamily members may expect you to make the adjustments for them, and thus the appreciation you are expecting simply is not there. As a result, you may feel disappointed and as though you're the one doing all of the work in the stepfamily.

If you believe that you're the one who must do all the adjusting, what can you do about this belief? The best thing is to understand what your ideas about your stepfamily are before you get into it. Be realistic about your expectations about your stepfamily members. If you have this particular belief, you can:

- Understand that wanting to make all of the adjustments yourself is a gracious and generous idea, but determine if it's really realistic for you. Can you really do all of the adjusting in the stepfamily and then not be upset if your spouse and stepchild appear to make none?

- Don't *begin* to do all of the adjusting in your stepfamily. If you start doing this, you'll only confuse things if you become frustrated and stop. Once you know the routines in the stepfamily, call a stepfamily meeting to discuss those routines that are causing problems for you.

- Be clear to your stepfamily members that *all* of you need to make adjustments to one another with regard to stepfamily routines.

Belief 2: The Stepparent Will Always Be the Outsider

This is a common belief for stepparents. Why? Because you've heard it from so many other people when they found out you were about to become a stepparent. The status of outsider has long been associated with being a stepparent. The dynamics of a stepfamily create this belief. For example, as a stepparent, you are joining a family that has already been in existence. You're coming in from the outside. Essentially, this makes a stepparent the outsider. But remember, if you believe it, you may become it.

Let's look a bit more closely at why so many stepparents have this belief. The first and most obvious reason is that everyone else in your immediate stepfamily is biologically related to one another. This automatically excludes the stepparent from any type of bonding that has already been established. Even though this reason is obvious, it's a very powerful point of conflict in many stepfamilies, particularly if a relationship is not begun and developed with other members of the stepfamily. Because a stepparent has the immediate sense of being the outsider, this status may become more intense as time goes on, particularly if consistent and unresolved conflict occurs in the stepfamily.

But why is being the outsider such a sensitive issue in the stepfamily? There are other situations in life where you will feel like an outsider. For example, the first day on a new job or attending a party with a friend where you don't know anyone. Think of a situation in your life where you felt like an outsider. Remember how you felt—uncomfortable, unsure of yourself and perhaps inadequate, wanting only to get out of there. But how do these situations differ from feeling like an outsider in the stepfamily? The biggest difference is that on the job or at a party, you aren't striving to become unconditionally accepted. Another difference is that the job or party situation doesn't last for a prolonged period of time. In the stepfamily, you want to be accepted immediately if at all possible. You also experience the status of outsider for a longer time in the stepfamily, and the longer it goes on, the more you begin to feel that you will *always* be the outsider. This feeling is consistent, and if it's a problem, you live with it every day in the stepfamily. This feeling of being an outsider begins to dominate your relationships, and it is at this point when it becomes problematic for you and your stepfamily. The feeling of being an outsider can be detrimental to you and your stepfamily, which is why it is important for you to understand it as a changeable belief and for you to know what to do about it.

What can you do if you have this belief? Try to understand that feeling like the outsider in your stepfamily is normal. Try to put it into perspective, however. Ask yourself these questions:

1. Do your stepfamily members really treat you like an outsider?

2. Is this simply your *perception* of the situation?

Only you will know if this is real or imagined in some way. As a result, you will be the only person who can change or fix this uncomfortable feeling.

Changing your uncomfortable feelings is yet another opportunity to be proactive in your stepparent role. This allows you yet another opportunity to be proactive in your stepparent role. How? By taking control of this feeling of being the outsider and working through it by following these steps:

Feeling Like an Outsider

First, identify why you feel like an outsider in your stepfamily. "I feel like an outsider because _____

_____

_____

_____

Second, discuss your feelings with your spouse. Explain why you feel this way and create two solutions that you and your spouse can do together to help you eliminate these feelings.

Solution #1 _____

_____

_____

Solution #2 _____

_____

_____

Belief 3: You Should Be Your Stepchild's Friend

You want your stepfamily to be successful, and you want to do every-thing you can to achieve this success. You may hold the common belief that in order to have a happy stepfamily, you must ensure that your relationship with your stepchild starts out on the right foot. This is a nat-ural and expected feeling. You think that pleasing your stepchild and becoming their friend will be a great way to get your stepfamily working together as a solitary unit. This is totally reasonable.

But shortly into the stepfamily-building process, you begin to notice that your stepchild is doing something that may require correction. Let's say that you're the only person at home when the stepchild needs disci-plining, and you do it. What happens? Your stepchild becomes upset with you. Why? Because up until this time you have been trying to please them, and they saw you as a friend—not as a parent who will cor-rect their behavior. What does the stepchild do? They go to their parent, your spouse, and tell them what happened—or at least their perception of the events that took place. You feel confident knowing that your spouse will support you in your behavior.

But you soon learn that your spouse is defending their child and not you. Suddenly there is conflict in the relationship with your step-child and your spouse that didn't exist before. You begin to feel that you shouldn't have said anything to your stepchild, and you may feel unsure about doing this again. But feeling this way hampers your desire to be a parent and equal partner with your spouse. You may also begin to think that this stepfamily situation is more complicated than you thought. You begin to feel disappointed, alienated, and stripped of your authority as a parent.

It's at this point that the belief that you should be a friend to your stepchild loses it's allure and you begin to question whether this step-family was a good idea or not. But what can you do about this belief once you are well entrenched into the stepfamily dynamics?

First, understand that many stepparents start out behaving this way with their stepchild. You will want to trust your stepchild, and that's great, but you must understand that if you start out being a friend and then change to "parent" without any warning, your stepchild will be confused. Invariably they will go to their parent to discuss this and prob-ably to complain about you. It is vitally important that when this occurs, that you be understanding with your stepchild and with your spouse and work through an amicable solution. Secondly, I'll suggest that it would be best to prevent this problem altogether. How? Recognize that you have this preconceived idea and change it. If you want to be a friend to your stepchild, do that. But if you plan to parent your stepchild, you must take a different route (which is outlined in the parenting team process described earlier in this book). Don't confuse the dynamics in the stepfamily. This creates conflict, and the last thing you want to do in your role is create conflict.

Remember that identifying and understanding beliefs is a great step toward avoiding pitfalls in your stepfamily.

Belief 4: The Stepparent Should Come First

We all want to be first with our spouses. Why should this be any different in our second and subsequent marriages? Because the spouses we marry the second time and beyond may have children, and the children will come first. Period. And that's the way it should be.

But what happens if you know this in your mind but in your heart you still want and expect to be first with your new spouse? The answer lies in the support you need and should receive from your spouse. It's not possible for you to be first while your stepchild is living with you in the household. But it *is* possible that your spouse can support you in ways that will help you feel that you are first to him or her. As the stepparent, there is not one single thing that you can do to be first, but you can appreciate the efforts your spouse is putting forth to help you feel number one, even though you can't be. Another way to deal with this issue is for you to accept that you simply cannot be number one while your stepchild is growing up and living in your home. Much of the stepfamily success is defined by the relationship that you have with your stepchild, and by being tolerant and patient in waiting to be number one, the chances of success in your stepfamily are greatly improved.

So what can you do if you have this belief? First, understand that it is not your job to achieve number one status with your spouse. Why? Because your spouse would put you first if they could, but they cannot. He or she has children and the children come first. Your job in this role is to understand and accept that you need to be patient and wait your turn. Another way to deal with this belief is for you to put your stepchild first. Put your energy into supporting your spouse in making the child first. Focus your role as parent on making your stepchild a priority.

By doing this, you will be not only showing support for your spouse, but deepening your relationship with him or her. Supporting your spouse's children's needs will be a wonderful way to increase the chances for success of your stepfamily.

Belief 5: Your Spouse Will Side Fairly with You and their Child

This is a common belief among stepparents, and if this were the case, stepfamilies may struggle less. Why do stepparents have this belief? Quite simply, we love our spouses and expect that they will defend us and support us in any conflict in the stepfamily—even conflict with our spouse's child. However, is this a realistic belief in a stepfamily? The answer is no, and if you exert frustrated energy about this, you may find that you are the only one in the family who is frustrated and a frustrated stepparent leads to an unhappy stepparent.

Why is this belief unrealistic? Your spouse will not want to believe that his or her child is wrong. And in the traditional family, less opportunity exists for a child to encourage a parent to take sides. But in the stepfamily, conflict between the stepchild and the stepparent will occur and perhaps often. As a result, your stepchild will go to their parent, your spouse, and your spouse will want to believe and defend the child. This is extremely common in stepfamilies, and if this is happening, don't be alarmed. Rather, focus on what can be done about the dynamic, because if it continues, you may begin to feel defeated and this will be harmful to your stepfamily.

What can you do if you have this belief? Understand the intense bond between your spouse and his or her child and do not underestimate this bond. Your spouse may support you in every other way in the stepfamily, but when it comes to their child, don't expect your spouse's support, at least not every time there is a conflict. Should your spouse be reasonable in defending and supporting their child? Yes. Can your spouse be objective when it comes to their child and what their child may be doing wrong? Maybe, maybe not. What should you do? Your role should be to act reasonably and understand your spouse's dilemma here. Be proactive. Rather than waiting to be surprised, hurt, and disappointed the first time your spouse defends your stepchild and not you, understand that this can and will happen. In time, when your spouse reaches a comfort level with understanding that you are not out to blame their child for everything that goes wrong in the stepfamily, they will likely be reasonable and support you when your stepchild has done something that needs correction. Be patient and in time, you will have a degree of control over this situation.

Belief 6: Your Spouse Will Make the Stepfamily Work

You will want your marriage to work. You will also want your step-family to work. You may count on your spouse to "fix" what goes wrong, particularly with their ex-spouse and with your stepchild. This is a natural feeling for any stepparent, and it kind of makes sense, doesn't it? After all, your spouse is the person that had a relationship with the ex-spouse and continues a relationship with their child. Wouldn't it seem logical that your spouse would solve problems that occur from these two parties? Logical, yes. Realistic—not exactly. But if this is not the case, then why do so many stepparents have this belief?

Well, for starters, you are the newcomer. You weren't there when your stepchild was born. You didn't know how the family functioned prior to the creation of your stepfamily. But your spouse *was* there. Your spouse has been in the family the longest. It's natural to feel that he or she will take charge and make sure that things go well.

But then what happens when you feel that your spouse is not taking charge and fixing the conflicts that erupt? In many stepfamilies, the stepparent then takes this role and tries to take action to fix things. But think of it—you're the one taking charge and trying to fix things with people who are relatively new to you. That doesn't make sense. But this role often seems to fall to the stepparent and can lead to the eventual breakdown of that stepfamily. What can you do in your stepfamily to prevent this from happening?

The first step to take is for you to understand that your spouse may not take the caretaker role. He or she may feel overwhelmed and unsure about how to handle the delicate balance between the relationships, particularly between you and the child. This role is difficult, and your spouse may feel that you will ultimately take charge and develop and/or fix your own conflicts with your stepchild. This is workable until your stepchild gets your spouse involved by taking their complaints about you to your spouse, their parent. But if you understand up front that your spouse may be unable or unwilling to become involved, you will reduce the disappointment with your spouse that you may feel down the road.

Another step that you can take if this was your belief is to talk with your spouse and determine together who will be the caretaker in the stepfamily. By working together on this, you and your spouse can work through conflicts as a team rather than risking the possibility of each ending up on the *opposite* side of a conflict.

Exercise: Explore Your Beliefs

Now let's look at examples of beliefs that you brought with you into your stepfamily. Each of your beliefs may affect your role as stepparent, and you need to examine them to understand why you react the way you do to certain incidents and events in your stepfamily. Reading through the more common beliefs above, you may have been thinking about your own belief system and how that has affected you in your role as stepparent. So let's try to uncover beliefs that may be hindering you from being the best in this role that you can, and want, to be.

Complete the following sentence.

When I married my spouse, I believed that our stepfamily would be

_____

_____

_____

_____

Has your belief come true? _____ Yes _____ No

Describe if the belief has hindered or helped your stepfamily and in what way. _____

_____

_____

_____

Repeat this exercise for other beliefs that you have. It's a good idea to revisit this belief system exercise periodically to ensure your belief system about your stepfamily remains positive and productive. I suggest that you review this exercise at least every six months.

Beliefs Your Spouse May Have

It's important to not only consider your own belief system, but that of your spouse as well. In my work with stepfamilies, I have found that the spouse sometimes is surprised or taken off guard by beliefs that the stepparent has about the stepfamily. Sometimes this has been confusing for the spouse because they aren't sure why the stepparent is acting or feeling a certain way. For example, if your spouse felt certain that you would know that she cannot always support your position in a discussion with their child, and you become upset when this happens, then it's pretty clear that your spouse is unsure of what you expected would happen in the stepfamily. And it's often these beliefs about how the stepfamily will function that can cause conflict, resentment, and tension in the stepfamily. So just as you are examining your belief system about your stepfamily, your spouse needs to do the same with honesty and clarity.

Exercise: What Are Your Spouse's Beliefs?

Interview your spouse for this exercise. This will provide excellent information for you as you build the Stepfamily Plan. This information will offer you insight into how your spouse sees the stepfamily working. The exercise will also help you understand why your spouse may say and do certain things that are confusing to you in the stepfamily. An example would be if your spouse remains neutral in an argument where they may know their child is wrong. Your reward from this exercise is invaluable insight into what your spouse is thinking. Explain about your belief system and ask your spouse to explain hers.

Ask your spouse to complete the following sentence.

When I married you, I believed that our stepfamily would _____

_____

_____

_____

Has our stepfamily met your expectation? _____ Yes _____ No

If no, why not?

_____

_____

_____

_____

What can your spouse do to change this?

_____

_____

_____

_____

What does your spouse expect *you* to do to change their belief?

_____

_____

_____

_____

Repeat this exercise with additional beliefs that your spouse discusses. This exercise will also help you understand what your spouse expects of you in your role. Having this discussion can be incredibly helpful, particularly if you and your spouse are unclear about expectations you each hold about the other.

You may also want to repeat this exercise with your stepchild. Doing this together with your spouse could provide insightful information, helping you and your spouse understand your stepchild's point of view on the stepfamily. This information could benefit the family significantly, particularly if you are experiencing conflicts with your stepchild. I would encourage you to record your discoveries in the following pages of your Stepfamily Journal.

My Stepfamily Journal

Chapter 4

The Real Story about Conflict in the Stepfamily

"Conflict." "Stepfamily." Two words that often go hand-in-hand. When stepfamilies initially form, the stepfamily members often expect some conflict and are prepared to deal with minor issues that occur. However, in my experience, the number of conflicts and the degree of difficulty in those conflicts surprises even the stepfamily members with the best of intentions for a successful stepfamily. The reality of the situation is that conflict can, will, and does occur regularly and over time in the step-family. In this chapter, we will discuss the different types of conflicts that occur in stepfamilies and explore real-life examples of this conflict and what it does to the stepfamily core.

Types of Conflict in the Stepfamily

There are two types of conflicts that occur in the stepfamily. One type is the day-to-day conflicts that occur out of what equates to strangers living in a home together. These occur primarily between the stepparent and the stepchild. Examples of these day-to-day conflicts include establishing a proper bedtime for the stepchild or enforcing the rule not to take telephone calls after 9 P.M. in the evening. This type of conflict can be relatively simple to resolve but does require agreement between the adults. Because the stepchild is the offspring of only one of the adults in the stepfamily, increased discussion and compromise may need to take place in even the less-complicated types of conflict.

The other type of conflict is more complicated and more difficult to resolve, and some of this type of conflict may not ever be resolved. Stepfamilies at times continue to move along even with this underlying current of conflict. What is this type of conflict and what can you do about it? This second type of conflict is ongoing conflict. The idea of ongoing conflict is not new to stepfamilies but sadly, ongoing conflict is a leading factor in the destruction of stepfamilies. Ongoing conflict takes its toll on each member of the stepfamily. It eats away at the core of the stepfamily, and the longer the conflict keeps on going, the greater the chances for stepfamily instability

Conflicts tend to last longer in a stepfamily. Why? Because conflict tends to go unresolved, cropping up again and again over weeks, months, and even years. This is difficult for anyone to understand who has not been involved in a stepfamily situation. After all, how can a conflict go on for years? The answer is simple. Conflict can go on for years because often the conflict in a stepfamily involves an issue that a bioparent cannot or will not compromise on. What is that issue that can become intransigent in the stepfamily? The issue is the children and what the bioparent is willing to do to bring about change in their child.

Some Examples of Ongoing Conflict

In order to demonstrate this kind of conflict more clearly, let's look at some real-life examples. In my work with stepfamilies over the years, I have come across a number of conflicts that occur regularly in stepfamilies and a variety of different ways that stepfamilies have dealt with these conflicts. In this next section, we'll take a closer look at these conflicts. Your job is to carefully read these examples and think about your stepfamily and any recent, current, or ongoing conflicts that occur in your stepfamily. Many conflicts that occur are similar across all types of stepfamilies; the factors may vary but the heart of the conflict may be the same. This information is intended to give you ideas of the similar conflicts that are present in stepfamilies. You may relate to the following examples and examining these issues may allow you to confront your conflict with a fresh, open-minded, and proactive approach. At the end of the chapter, you will have an opportunity to review the conflict in your stepfamily, step-by-step, through a problem-solving process.

A child's other bioparent doesn't want the new stepparent to "parent" their child. As with many ongoing conflicts in stepfamilies, this is an example of the problems between the adults in the complicated network of the stepfamily. In this particular example, the bioparent of the step-child does not want the stepparent to parent their child. This is clearly an unrealistic situation, and here's why.

The new spouse that the bioparent chooses is going to be involved with the stepchild. There isn't any other option. The stepparent will be living with the stepchild, at least at visitation periods, if not full-time. The stepparent's spouse will expect the stepchild to connect with the stepparent on some level, and the stepchild is going to expect some type of involvement with the stepparent. If the stepchild's other bioparent doesn't want the stepparent to have anything to do with their child, this creates significant conflict for the other bioparent and the stepparent. This kind of position on the part of the other bioparent puts the step-parent and bioparent in a difficult situation. It is not only unrealistic but unfair, not to mention that it sends a message to the stepchild that the stepparent is unimportant and someone not to be respected. Why? Because the stepchild's other bioparent doesn't think the stepparent is important or someone to be respected. This is clearly unacceptable and can be a huge stressor to the stepfamily.

Why is this type of conflict ongoing? Because it has the potential to go on for a very long time and may have little to no chance for resolution if the other bioparent chooses to assert this position over and over.

A disrespectful stepchild whom the bioparent does nothing to discipline. This conflict occurs more often than it should. Many stepfamilies have suffered immeasurable conflict and stress due to this very situation. Why would a bioparent allow their child to disrespect the stepparent— their spouse, the person they have chosen to spend their life with? It seems unbelievable, but in reality, it happens often.

Why would a stepchild disrespect a stepparent? There are many reasons. A stepchild may not like you and may try to demonstrate this. They may begin slowly with rude comments that are overlooked because you understand the stepchild is expected to make a huge adjustment. Unfortunately, the rude behavior continues to escalate. A stepchild may disrespect their biological parent, and have not had their behavior corrected, so they feel it's okay to do the same with the stepparent. Or, a stepchild may feel that if they disrespect you, then of course their bioparent will see that you are not somebody the stepchild wants around and the stepfamily will end. Whatever the reason, a stepchild disrespecting a stepparent is not acceptable—ever, anytime, anywhere.

To make matters more intolerable, the bioparent allows the disrespecting of their spouse to continue without parental intervention. Why would a bioparent let this happen? Don't they love their new spouse? Can't they see that their spouse is hurt by this? The answer is yes, they do love their spouse and yes, they see that this behavior hurts their spouse. So why let this situation go on? It often starts and continues for a number of reasons. Maybe the bioparent feels that the stepparent is the adult, and that their child doesn't really mean anything by it. Perhaps the bioparent is convinced that their child can do no wrong. Most probably, the bioparent feels that they caused their stepchild to be like this through the trauma of divorce, and that they should never have gotten divorced in the first place. In other words, the bioparent may feel helpless and not know what to do. This is understandable given that their job in the stepfamily is to find a balance between the stepchild and stepparent, not to choose one over the other.

In this situation, further damage is done by sending the message to the stepchild that the stepparent may somehow deserve to be disrespected for being the outsider.

The bioparent does not support the stepparent in disciplining a clearly misbehaving stepchild. As the stepparent, you will become a parent to your stepchild on some level and to some degree, depending on your comfort level and what your spouse wants to see happen. Often the stepparent feels uncomfortable in the role of disciplinarian because the stepchild is not your child—it's like disciplining a stranger. To add to this uncomfortable situation, if the bioparent doesn't support the stepparent in the discipline, it can create added stress, pressure, and dissatisfaction for you.

If you have a stepchild that misbehaves, you probably will feel it's your job to try and correct the behavior. You would want to do this independently of your spouse because you'd want the stepchild to learn to obey you and respect you in your role. This is reasonable. But if your spouse doesn't support your efforts toward discipline, you may experience conflict in a variety of forms—feeling alienated from your spouse, feeling like a failure in your role as parent, feeling like the stepchild is more important than you in the stepfamily, and feeling like your spouse doesn't trust your parenting decisions. This is a complex conflict. There are many ways this situation could impact you and the stepfamily, all of which are detrimental and harmful if not corrected.

What message is sent to the stepchild in this situation? Sadly, your stepchild receives the message that you are not the parent and that your efforts to correct their behavior are meaningless. This further alienates the stepparent and reinforces the idea of the stepparent as an outsider. If this conflict is ongoing, there is a point where it cannot be repaired, and the stepfamily is at serious risk for failure.

The stepchild doesn't accept the stepparent no matter how hard the stepparent tries to bond. This is a frustrating and energy-draining situation for you. You will want to bond with your stepchild because he or she is a significant player in your spouse's world. You will try everything you can think of to bond with your stepchild. Some strategies will work; some will not. But what if your stepchild just doesn't accept you, even after all you have done to make a connection?

Unfortunately this is a conflict faced by many stepparents. It's difficult to understand that your efforts to bond may be completely disregarded—and that does happen in some stepfamilies. As a stepparent, you probably expect at least some recognition from your stepchild—that recognition coming in the form of acceptance.

Your stepchild will have an opinion of you and you of them. You will feel expected to accept your stepchild as part of your role or duty as a stepparent. Your stepchild will not feel this same obligation. She or he may not accept you for a variety of reasons including feeling that you caused the breakup of his biological parents, feeling that you will leave if they make it clear that you're not accepted in the stepfamily, or feeling that they'll betray their other parent if they show acceptance of you. It's a difficult position for the stepchild to be in, and you most likely try to understand that. Can't your stepchild understand the difficult position you are in, too?

This type of conflict can be ongoing and last a long time. If it's not resolved, this conflict may cause significant problems in the stepfamily, including alienation of the stepparent and possibly the bioparent feeling pressured to make a "choice" between the stepchild or the stepparent.

The stepparent simply doesn't like the stepchild. Yes, this does happen. It's possible that you may simply not like your stepchild as a person. Your stepchild is not related to you and as a result, unconditional love likely is not present in this relationship. There are specific stepfamilies that do enjoy unconditional love between the stepchild and stepparent, but in general this is not the case. The conflict that occurs when you don't like your stepchild is serious and should not be taken lightly. This conflict has the potential for serious challenges to the survival of the stepfamily.

A stepparent doesn't set out determined to dislike the stepchild. The realization may come over time, with the stepparent experiencing a variety of emotions before realizing what the conflict actually is. Also the stepparent will go through agonizing guilt and frustration trying to understand the conflict and the source of this conflict. Why? Because you won't want to admit that you don't like your stepchild. This would hurt your spouse and possibly hurt the chances of your stepfamily surviving. It's difficult to admit that you don't like the offspring of your new spouse. You try everything you can think of to make the relationship with your stepchild work, and with each attempt, you experience failure. This most likely leads to alienation on your part, and can also bring up resentment when you see the closeness between your stepchild and your spouse. All of this builds increased tension within the stepfamily, and if the conflict isn't resolved, it could very well lead to the dissolution of the stepfamily.

If this is occurring in your stepfamily, you need to talk about it with your spouse. You need to work out a compromise on what is tolerable and comfortable in the stepfamily with regards to the contact you and your stepchild will have in the future.

Merging children that have been raised by completely different parenting styles. This certainly has the potential for ongoing conflict in the stepfamily. It's not likely that all of the stepchildren will respond to the same parenting style, thus modifying and adapting your parenting styles will need to take place. You may need to develop a parenting style that integrates the two the stepchildren are accustomed to, but don't necessarily expect full compliance from the children. This may become frustrating to you, so it's wise to be proactive and plan ahead for the frustration and how you plan to deal with it.

The problem with this conflict is that it will take a long time to work with and overcome in your stepfamily, if you ever do. It will require much time and energy from both you and your spouse plus the ex-spouse(s) to be successful. The stress created by this ongoing conflict may be difficult to deal with long term. The first issue to address prior to merging the parenting styles is to cease any disrespect toward the stepparent. This should not be tolerated by any stepchild toward any stepparent, no matter what the circumstances. The bioparent of the stepchild acting this way needs to step in and resolve the situation immediately.

Once that problem is resolved, you and your spouse will need to work on how to integrate your different parenting styles and the best way to merge the group. Merging your parenting styles will provide you the parenting consistency and guidelines needed to parent the stepchildren effectively.

The stepchild continues to sleep with the mother, then refuses to stay overnight at the father's house because she is expected to sleep in her own bed. This ongoing conflict occurs repeatedly in stepfamilies. Why? Often because one bioparent feels that allowing their child to sleep in the parent's bed will help their child feel more secure after a divorce. Sadly, at times it's because the *parent* needs to feel secure. They encourage the child to sleep with them, which becomes a habit, and this is quite a difficult habit to break. To many stepparents and bioparents, this situation seems unfathomable. However, it occurs frequently, and I have been asked about it repeatedly in my work with stepfamilies.

The problem comes in when the stepchild visits the other bioparent's house, and the stepparent and bioparent prefer the stepchild not sleep with them. However, the stepchild has been sleeping with their other bioparent in the home where they live, and when told at their other parent's house that they are to sleep in their own bedroom, the stepchild tends to panic. In extreme cases, the child refuses to stay overnight. As you are probably thinking, this causes many concerns in the stepfamily. If you let the child sleep with you and your former spouse doesn't, then your spouse cannot have their child stay overnight? If you continue this, when will your stepchild feel safe enough to sleep in their own bed? What if that never happens? What will you do then? This situation generates many questions and places the bioparent and stepparent in an awkward situation.

Plus, there is the concern of what this may be doing to the stepchild. If your stepchild is allowed to sleep with their other bioparent, is that creating a dependence in that stepchild on that bioparent? Would that threaten the relationship with your spouse and that child? If you say no to the stepchild sleeping with you and your spouse, will the stepchild blame you for this?

A stepchild that is clearly inappropriate and the bioparent looks the other way. Bioparents reacting to a divorce situation will sometimes allow their child to "adjust" to the divorce by not disciplining or correcting their child's behavior when they clearly misbehave. Bioparents will sometimes do this because they feel guilty about what they feel they have put their child through and don't want to add to the child's stress. What they don't often realize, however, is that children of divorce often adjust better than expected. The stepchild, sensing that they will now be able to get away with some unacceptable behavior, misbehaves more. Oftentimes this misbehavior is directed toward the stepparent because the stepparent is an "outsider" and often because the stepchild dismisses the stepparent's feelings.

This can quickly become an ongoing conflict if the bioparent continues to deny that it is happening or continues to minimize what this is doing to the stepparent's feelings. It can lead the stepparent to feel dissatisfaction with the relationship building with the stepchild, the stepfamily itself, and eventually the marriage. If you feel that your spouse is nonsupportive by continually allowing the stepchild to act disrespectfully, you may feel that all of your energy is going toward trying to fight the situation alone. What generally happens is the stepparent gives up— and understandably so. You begin to feel that you're fighting a losing battle, which you are. You begin to interpret this as fighting for your position in the stepfamily, which you are. This gradually feels unfair because shouldn't you be an equal partner in this marriage and stepfamily? The problems this conflict causes can lead to the destruction of the stepfamily quickly. If you are in this situation, it is imperative that your spouse understand their job in balancing the relationship between you and their child. It is their job to balance these two relationships in the stepfamily. It is also the bioparent's job to continue to correct their child's behavior and remain consistent in parenting even through the transition of divorce and into the adjustment period that stepfamily development requires.

A stepparent who refuses to allow a stepchild to continue to live in the stepfamily home. Believe it or not, sometimes stepparents do not permit their stepchild to live in their home with the stepchild's bioparent. To be fair to the stepparent, there may be very good reasons that the stepparent feels this is necessary. However, to make a ruling such as this is clearly not being a team player in the stepfamily much less being realistic. This situation has the potential to cause significant and long- term harmful results for the stepfamily.

First of all, this is a decision made by one person in the stepfamily. That in itself is not problematic immediately but does become a problem later. Why? Because it affects everyone involved in the stepfamily including the other parent. By not allowing your stepchild to live with you, you are denying your spouse access to their child, denying the step-child access to their bioparent, seriously harming the workability of the relationship with the ex-spouse, and hurting your marriage in the process. Once you make this type of decision, you risk creating long-term resentment, alienation, and hurt in your stepfamily and extended family. If your stepchild is a problem, I would encourage you to explore other, more suitable and reasonable ways to work through this. Making this effort would be the best thing you could do for your stepfamily. It is not your decision to decide where and when the stepchild lives. That is a parenting-team decision and something you will explore in detail in this book.

A stepparent that wants "instant authority." This is a common situation in stepfamilies and there are several reasons why it crops up so often. As a stepparent, you enter into a new family arrangement that suddenly gives you the opportunity for instant authority through a job as "parent." You want your stepchild to know this, and you want to give others in your stepfamily the message that you are an important part of this stepfamily and that you plan to take a significant role in decision making, including parenting. All of that is reasonable and realistic. How you handle this job and these new responsibilities is a good predictor of how the relationship and bonding with your stepchild will go, and will also predict the degree of conflict that will occur in your marriage about this.

If you rush in too quickly and too aggressively, you are likely to confuse your stepchild, and it will take longer to correct this in addition to easing any conflict you have with them. You also run the risk of your stepchild not trusting your approach, and that often takes a long time to correct. Your stepchild will look to their bioparent as their parent. They also may see you in this role, but it's likely that when you need to correct them, they will defer to one of their bioparents. If you become authoritative too quickly, your stepchild may rebel. Why? Because they see you as an extension of their bioparent, not of themselves. Their first reaction might be to tell you that you are not their parent and they don't have to listen to you. Or your stepchild may listen to you, but then complain to their bioparent about you. That places your spouse in an awkward position because they will feel obligated to talk with you about it and may feel they have to take sides.

What's the best way to prevent this before it becomes an ongoing conflict? Go slowly. Gradually and patiently, authority will come to you along with the respect and acknowledgment that you want and need in your stepparent role. Your needs will be met with time, patience, and a good deal of understanding—qualities a stepparent learns early to "stock up on" for the long journey into development of the stepfamily.

A stepson from one parent and a stepdaughter from the other parent become infatuated with one another. This is an issue that is becoming more common in my work with stepfamilies. Bioparents sometimes think about this before their families merge into a stepfamily; however, when it actually happens, the parents of each child feel helpless as to how to handle it. If the bioparents disagree over dealing with the situation, this problem can fester and cause significant concerns in the stepfamily. It is imperative that each bioparent understands this situation clearly and knows how they would feel if their biological child develops an intimate attraction for their spouse's. Then they can determine together how they would want to deal with it.

One of the first issues that needs clarification is to determine if this is an infatuation or if the stepchildren truly are in love. This will depend primarily on their ages. If the stepchildren are in their teens and this develops, it may be a crush that will pass. If the stepchildren are older, in their twenties or thirties, the possibility for intimate love may really exist. Some bioparents can accept this situation, but there are others who are unable to tolerate it. As a bioparent, how would you feel about your child falling for your spouse's child? Again, you may think beforehand that it would be okay, but once the situation happens, the bioparents may react quite differently to it.

The stepchildren involved may be fearful of telling you. This would be a situation that clearly needs to be discussed with the bioparents involved in the stepfamily because, if left hidden and unresolved, this relationship could grow into something that may prove detrimental to the stepfamily. This situation has the potential for long-term conflict for the adults and for the stepfamily members, including the extended family members.

An ex-spouse who controls the bioparent through guilt. Ex-spouses are generally a fact of life for stepfamilies. Adjustments will be necessary, coupled with a degree of patience, understanding, and tolerance on the part of all adults involved in the stepfamily. Expect this; it's a given. Ex-spouses certainly have their own issues that they're struggling with, just as you and your spouse do. This complexity can add to the tension and stress of having to deal with the person that married their ex-spouse and the new stepfamily their ex-spouse has created. Ex- spouses experience a variety of emotions, just like everyone else. Some of these emotions may include jealously and envy. Even as adults, we sometimes feel these emotions. That's normal, but it becomes problematic when these emotions spiral out of control and have an impact on others.

For example, if an ex-spouse appears to be controlling joint situations with the kids by using guilt with your spouse, it could become an ongoing conflict if left unresolved. Often what happens is your spouse doesn't like this dynamic either but doesn't know how to stop it, particularly if they've talked about it with their ex-spouse and he or she continues to do it. Then the pattern continues and after a while, your spouse decides to just live with it—which ultimately means that you live with it, too. It's an unhealthy interaction and may prevent appropriate parenting and decisions that need to be made. It also wears down your spouse emotionally, perhaps leaving them drained and not up for dealing with issues in the stepfamily. This type of ongoing conflict can cause significant concern in the stepfamily and interfere with proper parenting and guidance for the stepchild.

Every fight that you and your spouse have is over the children. I hear this often in my work with stepfamilies, and the stepparent is usually the one making this statement. If truly every fight you and your spouse have is about the children, then this situation is clearly a candidate for an ongoing conflict and could wreak significant damage to the stepfamily and marriage.

First, you need to examine if this is true. How would you do this? Keep a list of your arguments and what they are about. You may find that all of your fights are not about the children but are about different topics as well. I'm not suggesting this is good, but charting your arguments and the topic will help you get some perspective on just how often you argue and about what types of topics. Knowing this information will help you begin to problem solve the major issues of conflict in your stepfamily. If you do find that all of your fights are *not* about the children, then you will sense the exaggeration in the statement as well as its unfairness. At that point, I would suggest you examine why you would feel the need to categorize your arguments as only about the kids. For example, is it that you don't like your stepchild and the arguments are really about a bigger issue, such as you preferring that the children not live with you?

If you repeatedly suggest that all of the arguments are about the children when they're not, you may lead your spouse to wonder if the problem is with you and not the children. However, if you find in tracking your arguments that your arguments *are* about the children, I encourage you to take a close look at this and pinpoint the exact issue or problem. Once you identify the problem, you can begin to problem solve before this ongoing conflict becomes irreparable.

The bioparent continues to "rescue" the stepchild even when the stepchild needs discipline from their parent. This issue has come up several times in my work specifically as it relates to stepchildren reaching independence and young adulthood. Stepparents have expressed concerns about the amount of money and "hand holding" their spouses give to their child when in fact their child needs to recognize it's time to move out and become self-supportive.

One example of this conflict is when a bioparent consistently gives money to a child who is old enough and capable enough to get a job, live on their own, and support themselves. Other examples include bioparents allowing their young-adult child to remain living with them, even including a girlfriend or boyfriend moving into the stepfamily home, too. Extreme examples have included bioparents who have bailed their child out of jail repeatedly for delinquent behavior. As a stepparent, you will have the advantage of objectivity to see that this is not working for your spouse, but that it's working quite well for your stepchild! Your spouse may not be able to see this clearly and may feel she or he is helping the child by doing this. They are not. What your spouse is creating is the potential for intense ongoing conflict in your stepfamily and in your marriage.

If this conflict is occurring in your stepfamily, it may gradually reach a point where you become emotionally drained, give up, and the stepfamily disintegrates.

A stepparent who wants to discipline, and a bioparent who won't allow it. In general, stepparents want to take part in the disciplining of their child. However, there are exceptions to this rule. For those stepparents who want to take part in all responsibilities in the stepfamily including discipline, this conflict may crop up in your stepfamily.

Sharing the discipline is important; it cements your position in the stepfamily and helps support your spouse in their tough job as parent. Sharing the discipline strengthens you and your partner's marriage as a team, partnering together toward building a solid and healthy stepfamily. But what happens if your spouse is uncomfortable with you sharing the disciplinary role?

Initially this may be acceptable to you because you think you'll avoid your stepchild seeing you as the "bad guy." But gradually, by not participating in the disciplinary duties, you probably start to feel ineffective in your role as stepparent. Even though disciplining your stepchild is not always pleasant, it still can be an essential building block toward bonding—it creates a special portion of your relationship with your stepchild. If you are not allowed to participate in this function and can only watch from the outside while your spouse disciplines, you may begin to feel alienated from a very important and necessary part of working together as a stepfamily. You may begin to feel that you have less control in what happens with your stepchild and within your step-family. You may even disagree with the way your spouse disciplines, and this may frustrate you, causing tension and stress within the step-family home.

This could easily qualify as an ongoing conflict between you and your spouse that has the potential for damaging effects on your step-family and your marriage.

A bioparent that hasn't told their child about the stepparent before the marriage. It's natural for a bioparent to want to protect their child, espe-cially after a divorce. A bioparent may go to the point of dating someone without telling their child about the seriousness of the relationship or that they plan to marry this person. Oftentimes a bioparent will present their dating partner as a "friend" to the child, feeling this will avoid hurting the child and allow him or her time to understand and adjust to their parent having friends after the divorce.

When does this become problematic and conflictual? Often if a bio-parent feels they are dating too soon after the divorce but they've met this other person and feel the relationship is right. The bioparent then may feel that their child will think it's too soon. But trying to protect the child in this way is actually a source of future pain and confusion for the child, because when the person whom they know as their par-ents' "friend" suddenly becomes a stepparent, the child is taken utterly off guard. Suddenly this person has leapt from a friendship to living together in the same house, married to their parent! This can cause prob-lems for everyone—the stepchild because they may resent you and this "was all your idea." It can also be problematic for you because the step-child has not had the time to get to know you as their parent had. The stepchild may be leery of you and mistrustful because this all happened so quickly, and they've had little time to adjust to this idea.

This could become an ongoing conflict because, if the stepchild begins to mistrust you before the marriage takes place, it's likely that this distrust will continue in other situations while you are trying to build the stepfamily. This could also be a problem for your spouse because they will be dealing with a child that doesn't like or doesn't trust their parent's new partner. This is a difficult situation at best.

A stepchild that controls everyone in the stepfamily with his or her anger. At one time or another, it's likely you have dealt with an angry stepchild. This may be due to something they felt you have done or something one of their parents did. At any rate, stepchildren do get angry, even with your best efforts as stepparent. However, if a stepchild is angry about what seems like little things and for an excessive amount of time, this may be due to an underlying problem. As members of the child's stepfamily, you are the targets for this anger.

You and your spouse will not want to see your stepchild angry much of the time. Your reaction may be to dance around your stepchild in efforts not to antagonize them. This is understandable; however, it gives your stepchild the message that if they show increased anger, then they will have the power to control what happens to them—mainly that they will *not* be confronted with their behavior because they can intimidate you and your spouse. A bioparent may not want to discipline their child because they feel their child is already stressed enough. You may want to tread softly because you don't want to make matters worse. As a result, you and your spouse may be held captive by your stepchild's anger.

If your stepchild's angry much of the time and the situation appears to be escalating regardless of you or your spouse's efforts to correct their behavior, there may be an anger-management problem that needs attention. If left unresolved for fear of your stepchild's reaction, this may become an ongoing conflict for your stepfamily.

Okay, you're doing great. You have absorbed essential background information about your stepfamily, and you have a good idea of what you are working with in your stepfamily. This is exactly the foundation you need to start building your Stepfamily Plan, which we are going to start doing in the very next chapter. Your Stepfamily Plan will be created in stages, which are outlined in the following chapters. Please read the chapters carefully and complete the exercises honestly and completely. Remember, the more realistic you are about your stepfamily's conflicts, needs, and improvements, the more effective your Stepfamily Plan will be for a successful stepfamily and the more prepared you will be to deal with the issues facing you. So, take a breath, get a cup of cappuccino, and let's turn the page to begin the first stage of your Stepfamily Plan.

Part 2

Building and Maintaining
Your Stepfamily Plan

Chapter 5

Stage 1: Make Peace with Your Stepfamily's Past

Step 1: Accept the Past Family into Your New Stepfamily

Okay, you've married more than once. New spouse. New chance. They have a family; this is now your family. That's great, but wait a minute. This feels different from your first marriage. Yes, very different. There's you, your spouse, and all of these other people! Where's your privacy? Where are the romantic moments alone? Where's your influence in creating the kind of family you've always wanted? This family is already set up—and not really accepting new ideas or new ways of doing things. This is starting to feel uncomfortable. What have you gotten into?

Sound familiar? For your sake, I hope not. Sadly, this is sometimes how people begin in a stepfamily. So what do you do? Try to hide your feelings? Try to tell yourself a stepfamily really isn't like this? Or, maybe you feel it's just you. Everything will get better, won't it? But things don't always get better. In fact, small problems accumulate into large problems, and things escalate until you feel out of control. Why? Mostly because, as a stepparent, you have not historically held the position of a person considered to be powerful in the stepfamily. A stepparent has often taken the role of being the outsider and taken a back seat to the other, "real" family members. Even with the best intentions, the stepparent has rarely been taken seriously as a parent.

How can you avoid this kind of scenario in your stepfamily? After all, when you married into your stepfamily, your intentions probably were to assume an equal partnership with your spouse on all levels, right? Absolutely. That's completely reasonable. And congratulations on reading this book, because you are one of the progressive stepparents who is about to learn just how you *can* take charge of your role in the stepfamily. No more back-seat status. No more being considered an outsider. The only way to ensure the success of your stepfamily is for you to truly be an equal partner in your stepfamily. Accept that role; embrace it. You've taken a big leap forward.

To be sure your stepfamily survives and develops into a nurturing and healthy functioning unit, you need to do one thing. That's right, only one thing. What is it? Plan ahead. You're thinking it's much more complex than that, right? There are so many conflicts that can occur in a stepfamily that planning ahead might be impossible. Well, you're right on both counts. Your stepfamily is very complex, and it can seem monumental to plan ahead, particularly if conflicts are unpredictable. Or are they? In my work with stepfamilies, I have found that stepfamily conflicts can be predictable. Why? Because so many stepfamilies encounter the same types of conflicts, both day to day and long-term. And if you could predict conflict, and better yet, plan ahead to be prepared for the conflict, you could be a happier, calmer stepparent. Your relaxed demeanor would bring tears to the eyes of your stepparent friends. Other stepparents would want to know your secret. Really.

So, just how do you plan ahead for your stepfamily? Well that's easy. You create a working Stepfamily Plan, a vision of the future of your stepfamily. After all, you planned the wedding down to the smallest detail. Why not give that same focus and attention to planning for your stepfamily? In this book, this chapter and the chapters that follow will take you through the steps of creating your Stepfamily Plan. You will travel through the crucial development of your stepfamily.

Before we get into creating the actual Stepfamily Plan, let's talk for just a moment about what happens when you don't plan your stepfamily. Think about a party you are asked to plan, or a project at work that you are asked to manage. How about planning your investments for retirement? Whatever the project, think of an example that relates to your life. What would happen if you didn't plan for this event? Well, probably chaos. The people participating wouldn't know what to do because you haven't instructed them or given them guidance about what their roles could/should be. Without any planning, your project would lack a stable beginning—how would you or your participants know where to begin? Similarly, how would you know when the project was complete? Without proper planning, your project would lack direction and people would feel confused and probably become frustrated easily. This same scenario can play itself out in your stepfamily if you don't plan ahead. How? Your stepfamily members will be confused about what you are thinking and perhaps won't understand why you do certain things in a certain way. With confusion comes frustration, and with frustration comes a lack of commitment. Your stepfamily members may become disinterested in what your plans might be, and at that point, stepfamilies begin to break down due to a lack of clear vision and unity. Let's look at an example.

Quinn and Jesse were thrilled about their new marriage and the start of their new stepfamily. Quinn had three teenage girls and Jesse had two little boys. Quinn and Jesse both loved their children very much and they felt certain that when combined as a stepfamily their children were going to love living together and being a family.

Each feeling confident about their parenting styles and the family routines from their previous families, Quinn and Jesse didn't discuss specific details about their stepfamily and what would take place when. Both Quinn and Jesse felt that they knew their kids well, and they knew what to expect from them, just as the kids knew what to expect from the adults.

It was about nine months into the stepfamily when Quinn and Jesse started having arguments about each other's kids, specifically behaviors each of the children were doing that bothered them. Jesse felt confused and annoyed with Quinn's girls; why couldn't they be more tolerant of her boys? After all, the girls were older, and they should know better. Quinn felt that Jesse was too lenient with her boys and always found fault with the girls. It didn't take long to realize that this stepfamily was not on the road to stepfamily bliss.

How would this have been prevented? Simple. Jesse and Quinn could have sat down as soon as they knew marriage was the goal and started planning for the merging of their two separate families into one very special and workable stepfamily. Planning for teenage girls' and little boys' needs in the same stepfamily should be worked out prior to the marriage. Questions need to be asked such as, what happens if the girls get demanding with the boys? Who will confront the girls on this? Who will do the disciplining? Who will talk to the kids about what the adults expect? Make a list of your expectations of the kids. Share this with your children so they know what's ahead. This not only prepares you for conflict that will occur, but it also teaches your stepchildren valuable lessons in planning. This is a great mentoring exercise for your stepfamily.

What other things could Jesse and Quinn have done?

- Plan the space in the house for kids' bedrooms to prevent conflict or encourage cohesion—where will everybody feel the most comfortable?

- Talk about the personalities of the kids. Map out who may conflict the most and be prepared for how you will handle this as a parenting team.

- Above all, Jesse and Quinn need to avoid attacking each other. Jesse and Quinn are the captains of the team; they need to be supportive of each other. This doesn't mean Jesse and Quinn have to agree on everything. But it does mean that they need to know how they resolve conflict between themselves before they can resolve conflict between the kids.

- Hold the stepchildren responsible for their behavior. This is very important. Stepchildren will often say it's not their job to fix problems because they didn't want the stepfamily in the first place; their parent did. Don't let your stepchildren pass on this one. They need to learn valuable relationship-building skills, and a stepfamily is the perfect place to do this. Teach them. That's one of your jobs.

Step 2: Build the Stepfamily Plan

Now, let's talk about the basic overview of a Stepfamily Plan. Essentially, there are three basic elements to a good Stepfamily Plan.

- Merging the past into the present
- Defining the stepfamily member's jobs
- Knowing what obstacles to prepare for

Merging the Past into the Present

All members of the stepfamily come together with a past, whether that included a previous marriage with children or no marriages and no children. This past is important; don't ignore it or try to eliminate it. As a stepparent, you want to understand that your spouse had a previous family, but sometimes you'd really rather it just disappear. This is not a productive strategy. You must acknowledge your spouse's past and your own, but you must also accept it and take it one step further by incorporating it into your new stepfamily. Remember, too, that your stepchildren also have a past, and you will risk the future of your step-family if you choose not to embrace your stepchild's past, understand their past family, or understand how your stepchild feels about their family. Why? Because you cannot build a long-term Stepfamily Plan unless all of the members' histories are acknowledged and understood. Without this piece, you will create a Stepfamily Plan that may be based on inaccuracies and perceptions that simply don't exist.

In my work with stepfamilies, a common theme with stepparents has been to want to ignore their spouse and their stepchild's previous family. Why? Because as a stepparent, you want your spouse and your stepchild to participate in this new stepfamily with you—and to leave the other family behind. You may feel threatened by their previous bond and family history together, that somehow that other family may pre-vent your stepfamily from being happy, successful, and fulfilled. In fact, the opposite occurs. If you ignore their family history, you will eventu-ally be *excluded* from real family bonding. Why? Because your spouse and your stepchild still have ties to that family, and they will be living with it on a day-to-day basis. If you reject this notion or ignore it, your stepfamily members will have little choice but to start leaving you out of the activities that involve their previous life, such as previous family hol-iday traditions, everyday household routines, or maybe family activities they enjoyed together.

Exercise: How Do You Feel about Their Previous Family?

Before we go further, stop for a time and think about how you really feel about the previous family your spouse and your stepchild lived in. Describe how you feel about this important part of their life. _____

_____

_____

_____

Now, do you feel your spouse and stepchild respect *your* past family?
Why or why not? _____

_____

_____

_____

_____

_____

Diana and Brent had been married just one year when they realized
something was wrong in their stepfamily. Brent had become increasingly
irritated with Diana's insistence on doing all holidays her way; in other
words, the way Diana and her previous family celebrated holidays.
Diana's rationale was that her children, Steven and Lexa, were accustomed to celebrating the holidays in the same way, and Diana did not
want her children to have to adjust to different traditions, such as the
way Brent's family did things with his children.

When I saw Brent and Diana in my office, the first thing we did was
specifically explore what the two family traditions were, their similarities and their differences. Brent and Diana made a list of what they felt
was important at family traditions, and surprisingly, their lists were vir-
tually the same. Both wanted their families to attend, both wanted the
same type of menu, and they agreed on the same day and roughly the
same time. So, where was the problem?

As we dug deeper into Brent's concerns, it became clear that this
conflict wasn't about family traditions as much as it was Brent's feeling
that Diana wanted to control all holiday celebrations by doing it her
way and ignoring what he and his kids wanted or how they did things
before. The couple didn't discuss this before they married, and Diana's
overprotectiveness of her children did get in the way of Brent wanting
to create new family holiday traditions. Diana had not been aware of
how this felt to Brent, and when she realized what his feelings were,
she was eager to get started on the assignment I gave them: working
out a plan for new holiday traditions that incorporated the old with the
new and making sure all members of the stepfamily could live with
that plan.

Exercise: Begin Merging the Past with the Present

So, you know what you need to do. But how do you begin?

To warm up and get you thinking, choose three issues from your past family that will impact your stepfamily such as:

- extended-family members

- ex-spouse (your ex-spouse and your spouse's)

- past family routines

- add your own

_____

_____

List ways each of the categories below affects your stepfamily:

Extended-family members: For example, your stepchild's grandparents, aunts and uncles are invited to the stepchild's birthday party, or you see the extended-family members at church.

Which extended family situations affect your stepfamily?

_____

_____

_____

_____

List one new way *you* will include the extended family into your stepfamily.

_____

_____

_____

Ex-spouse: For example, visitation schedules, telephone calls to your house for arranging things with the stepchild, see each other in town, or attending the same church.

Which ex-spouse situations affect your stepfamily?

_____

_____

_____

_____

_____

List one new way *you* will merge the ex-spouse into your stepfamily.

_____

Past family routines: For example, your stepchild will expect everything to remain the same; you may need to compromise on the way you do certain routines; you may feel alienated by past family routines; you may feel the past routines are forced on you.

Which past family situations affect your stepfamily?

_____

_____

_____

_____

List one new way *you* will incorporate your spouse and stepchild's past family routines into your stepfamily.

_____

_____

_____

By suggesting a new way to incorporate your spouse and step-child's past family into your new stepfamily, you will be rewarded with your stepfamily's happiness and they will be more willing to accommodate your needs. This is an excellent way for you to be proactive in making decisions for your stepfamily while preserving a piece of your individuality. So don't just incorporate the past family into your stepfamily, invite your past into your future. It's a winning step toward your stepfamily's future success.

Begin to Learn Each Stepfamily Member's Job

That's right, you not only have a job at work, but you also have a job in your stepfamily. Each member of your stepfamily has a job, too. It's not all up to you to fix everything and make everything better. It is the responsibility of every member of your stepfamily to do that. Great news, huh?

It's important that each stepfamily member fully understand their job and the specifics of that job in order to contribute to the success of the stepfamily. It's equally important that you and your stepfamily members understand that your jobs will change and evolve with each new year of development and growth within your stepfamily. Plan a family meeting to discuss your jobs. Write job descriptions for each member of your stepfamily. This will help remind your stepfamily members, and yourself, of your responsibilities in making your stepfamily the success it should be.

What Are These Jobs?

First, let's look at your job as the stepparent. In the first year of your stepfamily's crucial development, your job is to focus on your stepfamily and not on what everybody else is telling you. Why is this important? Because stepparents receive all kinds of advice from well-intentioned friends, family members, coworkers, and other stepparents. This information may not be accurate, however, and you need to respond to the realities of your particular stepfamily. Each stepfamily is unique and although similarities do exist as we discussed earlier, your stepfamily will be as individual as you are. You need to focus on that. Forget everything that everybody else told you. Only you will know how you truly feel and how you will direct and guide your stepfamily's future. Your experience may be quite different from the stepparenting horror stories you may have heard. Above all, be kind to your stepfamily the first year. Try to understand each of your stepfamily members and respect where they have been. You will want the same from them.

Now let's look at the bioparent's job. The primary duty of the biological parent in your stepfamily in the first year is to help you feel comfortable and find a place in the stepfamily. You may not know what your role is yet. Your spouse will need to support you and help you formulate that role. Your spouse must also help you form a relationship with your stepchild—this is not your job alone. It's the bioparent's job to help you and your stepchild create a bond.

The stepchild also has a job in the stepfamily. In the first year, the stepchild's job is to respect you and your role in the stepfamily as coparent and authority figure. This role may continually evolve; however, it is paramount that the stepchild accept and understand that at least a portion of your role will be as an equal and functioning member of authority in this stepfamily. It's also the stepchild's job to help you fit into their existing family and to cooperate with the development of the stepfamily plan. Stepchildren will often feel that they have no place— that they exist in the stepfamily only because their parent wanted this. Not true! The stepchild is a very important part of the stepfamily equation. However, with that ranking comes responsibility and that takes the form of a job—just like you and your spouse have.

Begin to Know What Obstacles to Prepare For

Okay, now let's take a look at the actual Stepfamily Plan. What is a Stepfamily Plan? Why is it important?

The Stepfamily Plan involves identifying the obstacles or conflicts that will confront you in your stepfamily and developing a solution to those obstacles so that you are prepared for them. Planning ahead allows you to practice your responses so that when the conflict does occur, you and your stepfamily members are not taken off guard. You will know what to expect, and by knowing what to expect, you can be ready with solutions rather than experiencing frustration and resentment. The Stepfamily Plan is also your vision of your stepfamily. What did you envision your stepfamily to be? What do you *want* your stepfamily to look like? Your stepfamily can be whatever you want it to be. All you need to do is plan ahead.

In the following chapters, you will be taken through an actual Stepfamily Plan listing specifics of what to expect and at what stage to expect it. You will have the opportunity to develop your own Stepfamily Plan tailored to your family.

Step 3: Create Your Parenting Team

Next, you will need to create your parenting team. Why do we need a parenting team? Won't your parenting skills and your spouse's be enough? The answer seems so obvious. Sure, your parenting skills and your spouse's should be enough, but it's just not that simple. In a stepfamily, you are parenting with more than one person. You are parenting with your spouse, but you also need to parent with your stepchild's other parent and with your child's other parent. That's a lot of people, and frankly, this combination can be overwhelming in a stepfamily for everybody involved.

I have discovered in working with stepfamilies that one of the reasons stepfamilies fail is because of the lack of continuity in parenting between all of the parents involved. The stress that results from the chaos of all of the parents trying to parent the same children—from a biological parenting perspective and from the stepparenting perspective—is difficult at best. This may work for a short period of time, but gradually the conflicts become frequent and reach a point where they simply cannot be resolved. The adults begin bickering and the stepchildren may start to take advantage. What happens? The adults wear out and the stepchildren lose interest. In my work I have used the strategy of developing a parenting-team approach to the stepfamily to help sort out this problem.

What Are the Benefits of a Parenting Team?

Developing a parenting team is beneficial in many ways, but specifically:

- It keeps all parents involved on the same path;

- It allows all parents involved to understand the parenting goals for the stepchildren;

- It allows a checks-and-balances system for the parents to keep each other informed *and* to monitor each other;

- It gives a clear message to the stepchild that all the parents are working together;

- It reduces the opportunity for the stepchild to manipulate or build a wedge between any of the parents.

Before you panic because you are certain one of the ex-spouses isn't going to go along with this, relax! Take a deep breath. Now, let's discuss how to make arrangements for cooperation in even the most delicate stepfamily situations.

In stepfamilies, the stepparent and the new spouse may have discussed how they plan to parent their children and stepchildren—and that's great. This is so very important to the success of the stepfamily. But even in the best situations, where the stepparent and bioparent have discussed this and have come up with a plan for their stepfamily, conflicts can occur from the outside—when the stepchild is parented by their other parent, the one that lives someplace else. The best of intentions can be achieved by the stepparent and bioparent, but if the stepchild's other parent is parenting in a completely different style, the stepchild:

- Needs to adapt to two or more parenting styles

- May find loopholes to work in their favor

- May find discrepancies and have an opportunity to build a wedge between the parents, which can cause destruction of the stepfamily

It's not the end of the world if your stepchild has to adapt to more than one parenting style. That's not the point here. What you do need to focus on is that if you parent with different styles, there is a greater chance of conflict between the adults, not the adults and the stepchild. When conflicts occur with the adults, ex-spouses included, the breakdown of the stepfamily slowly begins. Why? Because the adults who are supposed to be parenting tend to get so caught up in being angry or blaming the ex-spouse, or even the new spouse, that the stepchild may get lost in the shuffle. Follow-through on disciplinary measures and parenting requests may get ignored. That's not okay. The stepchild may soon figure this out and may even be able to predict when this breakdown will happen. Stepchildren are keenly astute at finding weaknesses in parenting styles and worse, at finding weaknesses between their bioparents and between their bioparent and you. It's your job as parents not to let this happen. One of the best ways to guard against this kind of opportunism is to have a solid, cemented parenting style that *all* of the parents involved agree to and utilize with the stepchild.

Monica and Jordan had been married for two years, and they both felt their stepfamily was going well. Sure there were a few problems, but nothing insurmountable. But there was a problem that was becoming difficult. That problem centered around Jordan's teenage son, Judah. Jordan and his ex-wife, Silvie, had parented Judah in two different ways. Jordan felt this was the reason for their divorce, and he knew that it may be a problem with his new stepfamily with Monica. Jordan was right. Jordan was the strict parent; Silvie was more lenient and felt that rewarding Judah with expensive gifts worked well. When Jordan and Silvie divorced and were living separately, they each continued to parent Judah in the same ways. Enter Monica.

Monica agreed more with Jordan's parenting style such as holding Judah accountable for his actions and giving fewer material rewards. Each agreed to reward Judah for the correct behavior with love and nurturing. While Monica and Jordan were parenting Judah in this style, Silvie continued to parent with materialism. Soon it became clear to Monica that Judah knew how to work this situation to his advantage, particularly at his mother's home. Although Judah wasn't allowed to have more than two friends over when Monica and Jordan were out for the evening, Judah decided to have a party with his friends at Silvie's one evening when Silvie was out for dinner. Silvie was upset about this, feeling that Jordan took advantage of her leniency. She discussed the party with Jordan, who in turn discussed it with Monica. Monica and Jordan were concerned. What message was Judah getting from his mom's parenting style? That he could get away with stuff with her mom that Dad doesn't allow at his house? This became a collective parental problem.

In my office we discussed Monica and Jordan trying the parenting-team approach. They talked with Silvie about this, and Silvie, frustrated at not knowing what to do with Judah, agreed to try the parenting team planning approach. Monica, Jordan, and Silvie began to meet twice a month over coffee. The initial meeting outlined what the parenting style was going to be, integrating input from all three parents, and ended with an agreement to keep the parenting style as consistent as possible. The subsequent meetings were to check in and determine whether the plan needed any fine tuning. Their parenting team rallied into action, and the results were very good. It was awkward at first, because Judah was comfortable in knowing how things worked before. Once Judah was parented similarly in both homes, the opportunity for conflict reduced significantly, the criticism between the parents reduced, and Judah had fewer chances to take advantage of a faulty system. Monica and Jordan also relaxed more because they didn't need to worry about Judah as much when he was with Silvie. It was a win-win situation.

Exercise: Creating Your Parenting Team

Identify the players: You, your spouse, and _____

_____ (the ex-spouses)

Schedule a series of meetings: Choose a neutral place such as a coffee shop or a casual restaurant.

First Meeting

In the first meeting, you will be discussing your parenting styles toward the goal of trying to develop one style that all parents can adopt for parenting consistency—for the stepchild and for the parents.

- Set a time limit of one hour.

- Discuss the different parenting styles used by each parent. Point out the strengths of each, not the weaknesses. This meeting is not a time to criticize another parent.

- Discuss developing *one* parenting style.

- Stay focused on what is best for the stepchild.

- Be fair; you called the meeting, but it doesn't mean you are in charge.

- Don't worry, you do not have to be best friends with the ex-spouses.

- Emphasize that this strategy is for the benefit of *each* parent.

Second Meeting

This is the meeting where you write a mission statement for your new parenting style. It could start something like, "As the parenting team, we will parent as a group. We have chosen and agree to . . ." After you have a suitable draft of your mission statement, it would be wise to make a list of the rules that will be consistent in each home. For example:

- Bedtime is 9:30 P.M.;

- No phone calls allowed after 9 P.M.;

- Meals will be eaten together as a family, particularly the evening meal;

- Bedrooms will be cleaned weekly.

- No friends allowed when the stepparent has book club night (or whatever might be specific to the stepparent/bioparents).

Agree on the basics. These are simply suggestions. Do be as specific as possible. Focus only on the rules that can be consistent in each household. This will depend on each parent's schedule, of course. Make a copy for each parent, and make efforts to follow this as closely as possible.

Third Meeting

This is a follow-up meeting to check in on how things are going.

- What do we need to fix?

- Focus on positives, discussing what is working well.

- Does having a parenting team affect the stepchild's behavior? If so, in what ways?

- Have we achieved our goal of reducing conflict?

Do regular follow-up meetings. Meeting once a month in the first two years will help you get the most out of your team. Then you can gradually taper off to one every three months, then twice a year, until you reach the point where no follow-up meetings will be necessary (unless you want them, of course!).

The point is to maintain consistency between households to help the parents reduce conflict with each other and with the stepchild and to allow your stepchild to feel that the two households work in unity. The greatest benefit is that you will be a fine role model to your stepchild in helping teach them how to positively parent for their future family (or stepfamily). This will be a time commitment on the part of each parent; no question about it. Do it—invest the time. It will be well worth it in the long run, and not only for your stepfamily's success. It will also enhance the harmony of your stepchild's world when it comes to juggling multiple parents.

One final note: Developing a plan and creating the parenting team as early as possible will reduce conflicts and give your stepfamily a greater chance for success. But for those of you who are veteran stepfamily members, there is still hope! It's never too late to get started on your Stepfamily Plan.

Now that you are the expert, use your skills wisely! Be a mentor to other stepfamilies that you know at church, at work, or in your community. Start a stepparent group and teach your members how to create their very own parenting team.

The following is a summary of the first stage and chapter regarding your Stepfamily Plan. Complete this summary about information specific to your stepfamily. You will find a similar summary after each subsequent chapter in the book. The purpose of the summary is to highlight the key points in the stages to help you stay focused on the information needed to help formulate and build your Stepfamily Plan. You will use this information by reviewing the summary information in the months and years after you have created your Stepfamily Plan to help your stepfamily stay focused and to "see" the progress that you've made. So, let's get started on completing your first summary with information specific to your stepfamily on accepting the past family into your new family, identifying the specific challenges you may face in building your Stepfamily Plan, and creating your all important parenting team.

Quick First Stage Summary

Step 1: Accept the Past Family into Your New Family
Check which rating applies to your stepfamily.

_____ Good job

_____ Need improvement

_____ I need help with this

Step 2: Build the Stepfamily Plan
What will be the biggest challenge in building your Stepfamily Plan?

_____ Getting my stepfamily members to do this with me

_____ Keeping focused on the critical issues

_____ Remembering to plan ahead!

Add your own:

_____

Step 3: Create Your Parenting Team

What will be the greatest reward for your stepfamily in creating the parenting team?

_____

_____

If you receive little cooperation, what should you do?

_____ Do not give up

_____ Create your own parenting team with the players who **will** cooperate

_____ Define and establish a parenting style for you and continue to evaluate with your spouse just how you are doing in this role

_____ Create a parenting support group with fellow stepparents whom you know

You now know how to accept the past family into your new stepfamily, identify some challenges you may face in building your Stepfamily Plan, and create your parenting team. Let's get into what to expect in Stage 2.

My Stepfamily Journal

Chapter 6

Stage 2: Observe, Listen, and Learn

Step 1: Learn About Your Stepfamily Members

In Stage 2 you will focus on getting along with your stepfamily members and do the following:

- Observe, listen, and learn—explore each other's habits and routines

- Don't try to fix everything at once; go slowly

- Continue to develop your stepfamily vision

- Be flexible, particularly with house rules in both households

- Expect problems; anticipate that everything will not be ideal or perfect

- Continue to write in your Stepfamily Journal

Your stepfamily should be focused on getting along with one another because once you know one another better, it will be much easier to add your input or expect your stepchild to obey you. This should not be anything intense; just casually develop an understanding about and for one another. You're exploring each other's habits and getting comfortable with routines that will develop in the stepfamily. One caution—don't try to fix everything at once. You're not trying to solve the world's problems the second month into the plan. Give yourself a break, and just enjoy your spouse and your stepchild. Your energy will need to be preserved for later, when more conflicts arise that may prevent you from enjoying your stepfamily members.

The second stage is critical to the success of your stepfamily. Why? Because the second stage is where you need to establish the major cornerstones of the stepfamily. But what if your stepfamily has been together for years and you haven't yet built a Stepfamily Plan? Relax—it's never too late. The Stepfamily Plan can be started at anytime, no matter how long you have been a stepfamily. The cornerstones, guiding principles, stepfamily vision, and the obstacles laid out here will apply to all stepfamilies no matter what step you're in. The key is to get started as soon as you can because the sooner you begin, the sooner you will enjoy the rewards of planning your stepfamily.

So, what are these important cornerstones in your stepfamily's development? Well, we discussed several in chapter 5, so let's review briefly. The first cornerstone is to accept the past family into your new stepfamily. The second is to commit to building the Stepfamily Plan together with your stepfamily members, and the third is to create your parenting team. There is, however, a fourth cornerstone and that is a strong and solid marriage. These are the most important tasks that you need to focus on in this second stage. Why is it essential that this be done in the second stage of development? Because you need to set the foundation for the future of your stepfamily's success. These four cornerstones will provide a basis for the major issues that will present obstacles to your stepfamily. By putting them in place, you will be taking the steps toward prevention of major conflict affecting your stepfamily *and* you will prepare your stepfamily to handle any future challenges by planning ahead.

There are several issues that need to be addressed in the second stage. In addition, there are several guiding principles that you should be aware of and that you should keep in mind. Let's review these guiding principles.

- Focus on your marriage. You need to cement your marriage and your commitment to each other. Why? Because the strength of your marriage will be a strong predictor of success in your stepfamily.

- Learn about your stepchild but don't make the stepchild liking you the priority. Help your stepchild accept your marriage to their parent first—there will be time for your stepchild to accept, like, and hopefully love you later.

- Don't be concerned with being the greatest stepparent in the world—that will come later.

- The second stage is about observation. Observe your stepfamily members and they will be observing you. You are learning about each other. You must have this background information before you can move ahead. Allow your stepfamily this time to just watch, listen, and learn. Even if you are starting the Stepfamily Plan after you've been together several years, you can begin again and take the time to observe your stepfamily members. As part of this project, you will learn new things about your stepfamily members that could help you understand more about specific conflicts that you are unable to resolve right now. Give yourself the gift of time spent getting to know each other all over again, and in a new light.

- Relax and slow down. This is not a race. You need to move slowly so that you absorb every important detail about your stepfamily.

Step 2: Stepfamily Vision

Before you embark on the journey to discovering what the second stage will bring in your stepfamily, it's imperative that you understand the concept of a "stepfamily vision." What is it?

Well, imagine that you are taking a trip to a distant land. Actually, this is your dream trip, something that you've wished for all of your life. You've planned it in your mind in such detail that you know how every minute will be spent. You know exactly what this trip should be, where it will be, what activities you will do there, and what the scenery will be like. The dreaming that you did about your trip was your vision—it's what you expected and wanted the trip to be. This vision about your dream trip is the same concept that applies to your stepfamily. You need to have a stepfamily vision, a dream or plan about what your stepfamily should and will be. Many stepfamilies do not have this vision—they simply start living together as a stepfamily and expect and hope that their stepfamily will be successful. Without a vision for your stepfamily, how would you know if your stepfamily is meeting expectations and heading toward the successful finish line? How would you know if you've reached your goal?

Important Components of a Stepfamily Vision

- A desire to be successful as a stepfamily

- Solid expectations of what each stepfamily member's role will be

- Knowing where you see your stepfamily in one year, five years, and ten years

- Confessing your commitment to one another and to the step-family as a whole

- Understanding that you will work through any conflict toward resolution and not give up

- Knowing what your role as stepparent should and will be in your stepfamily

As the stepparent, why is it important that *you* have the vision for your stepfamily? Because you are one that will pull your stepfamily together. You are the one who will orchestrate the team-building efforts in your stepfamily because this will be your project. The other members of your stepfamily have their family history already in place. You are invited into this already-existing family. That's great, but for you to have a stake in this family, you need to establish and build your own step-family—that includes you, your spouse, your stepchild or children, and their past family history. Your stepfamily members may feel their past family is enough—what they may not realize is that you may need more. You need and want your own family, the stepfamily, so that you all begin on equal footing for the long journey into the future. You want to move ahead together as one unit, not as the separate entities you were before you entered this stepfamily. What are the stepchild and your spouse's responsibility in this? To participate, cooperate, and help you build the Stepfamily Plan.

Case History: Lily and Jason

Jason and Lily were happy to finally be married and excited to start enjoying their combined families as their own stepfamily. Lily had so many ideas for her new stepfamily. She wanted the kids to like each other and do things together. Lily felt that life as a stepfamily would be a dream.

With Lily's enthusiasm, she started immediately to make suggestions to her stepchildren about what she would like to see them do in their spare time when she noticed that they sat around and watched TV a lot. Her kids were usually outside doing something or in their rooms studying. Lily felt her stepchildren needed her guidance to help them be more like her own kids. It didn't take long before her stepchildren started to resent this. Why? Well, they wanted to watch TV, and they weren't interested in changing their routines just because they were in a new household. Her stepchildren complained to their dad, Jason, about this but when Jason broached the topic with Lily, she was hurt and felt offended. This whole dynamic developed in only two months. What could Lily have done differently to prevent it?

First, Lily, as the stepparent, needs to slow down. Yes, your stepchild is going to do some things that irritate you. Expect this. It's normal. But just as you need to expect this, you also need to be prepared with how you will handle this with your stepchild. Should you start telling your stepchild what to do? That's easy—no! The best way to get your stepchild angry with you right off the bat is to start telling them how *you* think they should act or what they should be doing. The moral here? Don't come into your stepfamily and start controlling or "fixing" things. You are the outsider, remember? You need to ease into a position of taking charge in your stepfamily. The stepchild and your spouse need to adjust to the role that you are going to have. Don't push them into it.

Instead of jumping right in to fixing things in your stepfamily, take the opportunity to observe, listen, and learn about your stepfamily members. What should you observe, what should you listen to, and what will you learn? You need to observe your stepfamily members interacting with one another in your home. Who gets along best? Is there any obvious friction between any of the members? This will be important to you in the future because you will be able to plan ahead and prevent any major problems between the stepfamily members that conflict.

A major observation you need to focus on will be your stepfamily's strengths and weaknesses. Let's look at examples of strengths and weaknesses in your stepfamily.

Exercise: Strengths in Your Stepfamily

Check off the strengths that apply to your stepfamily, and add any additional strengths in the space at the bottom.

_____ We are all together most evenings

_____ We respect one another

_____ We basically like each other

_____ We all talk together at mealtimes and we share information easily

_____ We are nice to each other

_____ We enjoy doing the same things

_____ The parents alternate routines with kids, i.e., you and your spouse help one another in picking the kids up from soccer practice and attending school events

List your stepfamily's additional strengths: _____

_____

_____

_____

_____

Now let's take a quick look at what you observe as potential weaknesses in your stepfamily.

Exercise: Weaknesses in Your Stepfamily

_____ We rarely see one another

_____ We don't greet each other when one comes into or leaves the home

____ We don't do activities together—the adults are together but the kids isolate

____ We seem to breeze by one another without noticing

____ We don't ask each other about how their day went

____ We avoid each other

Where does your stepfamily need a little help? _____

_____

_____

_____

_____

Why is it important to observe strengths and weaknesses? Because you will be able to chart your progress in each of these areas from the start of your plan to see how successful your stepfamily will become. It's vital that you chart your progress in your Stepfamily Journal to determine if your vision for your stepfamily is coming true.

Step 3: Check In on the Conflict Level

Remaining flexible, expecting problems, and anticipating that there will be difficult days ahead are absolute keys to building a successful Stepfamily Plan. These concepts will help you understand that your stepfamily is not perfect and that you must be realistic about the chance for conflict in your stepfamily and the frequency of conflict. Stepfamilies experience more conflict generally than traditional families. The reasons are clear—you are combining virtual strangers together and expecting this combination of people and personalities to work. And when it doesn't, stepparents become frustrated and feel distant and isolated from the family. How do you prevent this in your stepfamily? Expect the unexpected. Build space and preparation for disappointment into your Stepfamily Plan. Emotionally you and your stepfamily members need to accept that conflicts will occur, and you need to be prepared to cope with this. What is the best way to prepare yourself? Call a family meeting and discuss it. Put it right out there on the table. Inform each member of your stepfamily that:

- Your stepfamily will experience conflicts, problems, and uncomfortable moments;

- You are being proactive in talking about this now, *before* any major problem happens;

- You're planning ahead as a team to know how to cope with problems once they start.

Exercise: How Do We Deal with Conflict?

List how each stepfamily member deals with conflict. Describe briefly how each of you react when problems come up. For example, "When I become angry or frustrated, I withdraw from everybody and eat." Now, you give it a try and also ask your stepfamily members to add their input.

Stepparent: When I become angry or frustrated, I _____

_____

_____

Stepchild: When I become angry or frustrated, I _____

_____

_____

Bioparent: When I become angry or frustrated, I _____

_____

_____

What will this information tell you? Knowing how each member of your stepfamily reacts to conflict, problems, or a crisis will help you all to understand each other better *during* an actual conflict and will prepare you to know what to expect from one another. Who will be supportive when you need it? Who will withdraw? Who will be loudly vocal or maybe even hurtful? Knowing this in advance will save you and your stepfamily members the painful experience of making judgments about one another and feeling the disappointment that accompanies the conflict. So be flexible, expect the unexpected, and anticipate problems, but be prepared with a stepfamily coping strategy such as this book and your Stepfamily Plan. By doing this, you will be light-years ahead on the problems you'll face, and you will be rewarded handsomely with a happy and well-adjusted stepfamily.

Step 4: Be Honest about Alienation

Do an emotional barometer check on feelings of alienation. What is alienation, why does it occur, and what should you do about it? Alienation is a common feeling that stepparents often feel as the result of being the outsider in an already established family. Alienation is feeling that you are being ignored or left out of your stepfamily, that you don't really belong. It is natural to feel a bit alienated in your stepfamily, and if you plan ahead for this, your reaction is much different and your ability to conquer alienation is much greater. Why? Because you will be prepared for an emotion that often takes stepparents off guard. Once stepparents become aware that they are feeling alienated, it's usually associated with embarrassment and shame, two emotions that prevent stepparents from working on the alienation. By planning ahead, you will be able to identify alienation and already have a plan in place for dealing with this.

Let's plan ahead for it now. Are you feeling alienated?

- Do you feel like your stepfamily members exclude you from conversations?

- Do you feel like your spouse and stepchild are ignoring you?

- Do you feel as though your spouse and stepchild do things without you?

- Do you feel that your spouse makes all decisions without you?

- Are you isolating yourself? Spending more time alone?

These are all signs of feeling alienated and isolated from your stepfamily. If any of these are occurring, you must do something about it now! Do not wait on this. Alienation only increases and often leads to the destruction of a stepfamily. But you can prevent this!

What should you do if you feel alienated?

- Talk with your spouse. Explain how you are feeling.

- Try to pinpoint exactly when you started feeling this way. By doing this, you will know how you felt before and how you felt afterwards. This helps you understand what *changed*.

- Was there one event that caused this alienation for you? If you can determine the cause, you can then begin to fix it.

- With your spouse, you must create a plan to deal with the alienation, such as:

  a. Your spouse will be more sensitive to your feelings and more supportive to you;

  b. You and your spouse will tell your stepchild together how you are feeling, and your spouse will be supportive of you during this conversation;

  c. Once a week, your stepfamily will take time to discuss how you are feeling and find out from you what they can do to help you through it;

  d. You will make a valiant effort to acknowledge your stepfamily's efforts to help you, and you will work at changing how you feel;

  e. Alienation is a stepfamily problem. It is not just *your* problem. You must all help to solve it.

One really healthy way to prevent alienation is to establish a routine stepfamily activity to do together—plan a regular stepfamily outing. This can be monthly, quarterly, or you can make it an annual. The point is to plan an outing together that you do regularly to *prevent* any further alienation. How? By you taking charge of this plan, it cements your position in this regularly scheduled activity with your stepfamily members and ensures your inclusion in a newly established stepfamily routine. Another healthy way to prevent alienation is to increase your interaction and bonding with your stepchild. During the early stages of the plan, you must continually increase your interaction and bonding with your stepchild because this will be a lifelong relationship-building experience for you. The success of bonding with your stepchild will predict the depth of your relationship with your stepchild for the future.

Remember to keep writing in your journal.

Let's stop a minute and evaluate where we have been in this chapter. How are you doing with the information? Are you getting a good picture of what needs to be done in your stepfamily? As you read these pages and absorb this information, I want to provide you with interactive guidance and assistance. I invite you to visit my website at www. docsuzen.com, where you can contact me with questions, concerns, or do problem-solving strategies for your stepfamily.

Congratulations, you've made it through the second stage! Time to evaluate how you and your stepfamily members did in this stage together. Let's do a quick review and summary.

Quick Stage 2 Summary

Step 1: Learn about Your Stepfamily Members

What did you learn about your stepchild? _____

_____

What did you learn about your spouse? _____

_____

What did you learn about you? _____

_____

Have You Written in Your Journal?

Go back and review your journal. What surprised you the most about your second stage together as a stepfamily? _____

_____

_____

Surprises can be valuable to your Stepfamily Plan. They offer you an opportunity for challenge and change. Take advantage of it! Be aware of strengths and problems as you review your second stage stepfamily history to note where problems still exist and/or where problems have been successfully resolved.

Rating Scale

Check off one.

____ Excellent—you feel confident about where your stepfamily is headed

____ Good—you have a few glitches but feel like you're making progress

____ Fair—you've made some progress but feel a little shaky

____ Poor—you need more work in the following areas:

What can you do to learn about your stepfamily members?

a. Talk to your stepfamily—find out what you can do *together*

b. Contact me at www.docsuzen.com

Step 2: Stepfamily Vision

Do you have a vision for your stepfamily? Check all that apply.

_____ A desire to be successful as a stepfamily

_____ Solid expectations of what each stepfamily member's role should be

_____ A sense of where you see your stepfamily in one, five, and ten years

_____ The ability to confess your commitment to one another

_____ An understanding that you will work through conflict toward resolution

_____ Knowledge of what your role as stepparent should be in the stepfamily

Check off one to rate your experience with stepfamily vision:

_____ Unsure about this   _____ Very uncomfortable with this
_____ Great, we put it all together

Describe *your* experience with building the stepfamily vision for your stepfamily: _____

_____

_____

_____

Who will take responsibility for making this vision happen? Check one.

_____ You   _____ Your spouse

Step 3: Checking In on Conflict

Check one.

_____ Few concerns here

_____ More conflict than I'd like to see, but manageable

_____ Horrible—there is constant conflict

What one thing can you do today to help reduce the conflict in your stepfamily? _____

_____

_____

Let's do a quick check on how the bonding is going with your stepchild.

Evaluate yourself here. Satisfactory _____   I'd like more bonding _____

What can you do today to improve your relationship with your stepchild?

    a. Talk more with your stepchild

    b. Show your stepchild how much you love their parent

    c. Prepare their favorite meal

    d. Today I will improve my relationship with my stepchild by _____

       _____

       _____

Your Stepfamily Activity

What's your regular stepfamily activity? Some examples could be an annual football game, a weekend a year at a cabin up north, a weekend at the beach.

_____

_____

Rating Scale

_____ Excellent—you feel confident about where your stepfamily is headed

_____ Good—you have a few glitches but feel like you're making progress

_____ Fair—you've made some progress but feel a little shaky

_____ Poor—you need more work in the following areas:

_____

_____

_____

Step 4: Alienation

Where are you currently with feelings of alienation? Check one.

_____ I have a handle on it

_____ It's there but not as much

_____ I feel very alienated

What can you do?

  a. Seek a stepparenting support group

  b. Seek professional help—alienation can be a serious stepfamily problem

What increased activities are you doing with your stepchild?

_____

_____

_____

Rate Your Stepfamily

_____ Excellent—you feel confident about where your stepfamily is headed

_____ Good—you have a few glitches but feel like you're making progress

_____ Fair—you've made some progress but feel a little shaky

_____ Poor—you need more work in the following areas:

_____

_____

_____

What can you do?

  a. Talk with your stepfamily members and problem solve together

  b. Seek support from a stepparenting support group

What are the most important basics that must be achieved in the second stage?

- Learning about your stepfamily members
- Checking in on the conflict level in your stepfamily
- Clarifying your stepfamily vision
- Understanding and dealing with alienation

When you've done your second stage work, don't forget to reward yourself. Take a break, buy something special for yourself, or have a double mocha decaf cappuccino. You've earned it. But remember, the greatest reward is that you have established the basis for your role in your stepfamily, and you are moving forward toward a successful and long-surviving stepfamily.

My Stepfamily Journal

Chapter 7

Stage 3: Assert Your Role in the Family

Okay, you've survived the second stage in the plan. Now you're ready for more, right? You bet. Let's get into the third stage of your Stepfamily Plan. You will be very busy in this stage, so take a deep breath and get ready for an adventure.

In Stage 3, you will increase your level of authority as stepparent of this stepfamily. Why now? Well, the second stage gave you an opportunity to get to know your stepchild better, learning what they respond well to and what parenting methods would not be successful. Be sure that you have covered these topics and that you feel comfortable and ready to move on. It will be important that you have a clear understanding of disciplinary styles that have been successful with your stepchild. You also worked on the parenting team in Stage 1, and this allowed you into the private chambers of the coveted role as "parent." Now you are going to assert yourself and become a more visible parent, role model, and disciplinarian to your stepchild.

Step 1: Take the Discipline Challenge

When I work with stepparents, the topic most commonly asked about relates to discipline. Questions such as,

1. "When should I start to discipline my stepchild?" and

2. "Should I parent my stepchild at all?" or

3. "How harsh or lenient should I be with my stepchild" are common.

It's the number-one issue on stepparents' minds. It may be your priority also. If not, it should be.

In Stage 3, this issue of discipline becomes more obvious in your stepfamily. In Stage 2, you practiced discipline to get a feel for it. In this third stage, you become a parent, one of the disciplinarians. If your palms are sweaty, it's okay. This isn't going to hurt. It may get sticky and sometimes complicated, but you've come to the right place to obtain guidance and direction on this incredibly important stepparent responsibility.

Discipline is a personal issue with stepparents, and prior to any action on this, you need to be sure that you have a desire to participate in disciplining your stepchild. Not all stepparents discipline, and you do have a choice in this. Some stepparents do leave it up to the bioparent. There isn't a right or wrong answer. You and your spouse need to decide what role you will take, if any, and you will also need to proceed with a plan if you do decide that disciplining is for you. If you don't participate in the disciplining, you need to be cautioned that if the stepchild does something you dislike or feel needs correcting, you will need to approach your spouse about it. If you have agreed not to discipline, you take the responsibility of living with your spouse's decision on how to handle situations with the stepchild in your home.

How to Effectively Approach Discipline

Let's talk about the correct and incorrect ways to approach this sensitive subject. The first thing that needs to be in place is the permission from your spouse to participate in disciplining their child. It is your spouse's decision to allow you to discipline their child, just as you need to grant your permission to your spouse if they will be a disciplinarian to your child (if you have children, that is). Why do you need your spouse's permission? Simple. It's respectful and the right thing to do.

Your spouse will naturally be concerned and maybe hesitant in allowing another person, an outsider, if you will, to discipline their child. Up until this time, only your stepchild's biological parents have probably done the disciplining, unless the stepchild has or currently lives with another stepparent. Your stepchild will need some preparation for your new authority, and so will the bioparent(s). If you have not discussed this *thoroughly* with your spouse, then I encourage you to do that before you begin any type of disciplining with your stepchild. In my work with stepfamilies, I've seen cases where stepparents have gone ahead and immediately started to discipline their stepchild without bioparent approval, which has led to problems not only between the stepparent and stepchild, but has seriously harmed the relationship between the adults. So before you do any disciplining, please consult your spouse.

Exercise: Is Your Spouse Prepared?

Here's a quick checklist for your spouse to consider prior to you disciplining. Circle "yes" or "no."

1. Is the bioparent ready for you to discipline   yes   no
   his child?

2. Has the bioparent agreed to let you discipline?   yes   no

3. Do you agree on how you will discipline his child?   yes   no

4. Do you agree on situations that require discipline?   yes   no
   For example, if the spouse feels his child should
   be disciplined for talking back, do you agree?

5. Do you agree on age-appropriate discipline   yes   no
   techniques?

6. Do you completely understand how the bioparent   yes   no
   has disciplined his child so that you have a
   familiarity with what the stepchild is used to?

7. Add any concerns your spouse has about this and be sure to discuss
   it *and* agree on a workable solution:

_____

_____

_____

_____

_____

_____

Discipline Missteps

Now, what is the incorrect way to approach discipline with your stepchild? The most common mistake you can make is to jump in too soon and start disciplining before the stepchild has a chance to know you as a person. Your stepchild must learn to trust you, just as they need to learn to trust other adults such as teachers, youth leaders, or pastors. You cannot and should not expect your stepchild to trust you immediately even though this may be what you think should happen as soon as you marry their parent. You need to earn your stepchild's trust just as they need to earn yours. Does this seem unfair? Maybe, but remember the dynamics of the stepfamily—you are a relative stranger to your stepchild. They didn't fall in love with you, their parent did. The correct way to move ahead with discipline is to give your stepchild time to know who you are and what they can expect from you. Then, you can start to be their disciplinarian.

Ellie and Jonas' Story

Jonas and Ellie were married after a short courtship. Ellie did not have children and Jonas brought two young boys, Dane and Gregory, to the marriage. Ellie liked the boys; however, she felt a little nervous around them. Ellie was unfamiliar with parenting, and she had no idea whether she would do it well.

Dane and Gregory visited every other weekend. Ellie became very accustomed to having a quiet home with just her and Jonas. When the boys arrived, there was usually lots of action, including noise and physical activity because the boys, who were six and seven, would wrestle around in the living room, bedrooms, or anywhere in the house where they happened to be at the time. When Jonas wasn't home, Ellie chose to discipline the boys when she felt they misbehaved. Initially, the boys would listen to Ellie—the boys really didn't know Ellie, and they showed a respect for Ellie that she was pleased with. However, gradually the boys started to ignore Ellie's attempts at parenting. This not only confused Ellie, but also annoyed and frankly angered her.

By the time Ellie and Jonas had time to discuss the situation, Ellie's feelings were at a critical point. Ellie had waited to tell Jonas how she felt because she didn't want Jonas to feel that she had failed as a parent with the boys. Ellie wanted to try different strategies at parenting the boys on her own. The problem was that the boys were continuing to misbehave. They had even started telling their other parent about "weekends at Dad's house," particularly that they didn't like the way Ellie "yelled" at them. By this time, Jonas was hearing from his ex-spouse about it.

What could have been done to change this situation? Several things:

- Ellie should have talked with Jonas right away about what was happening.

- Jonas and Ellie needed to discuss parenting *prior* to Ellie trying it on her own.

- The parenting team needed to be in place to prevent this from happening.

- Maybe a parenting class for Ellie would have helped.

- Jonas needed to make Ellie's role as parent clear to the boys first.

Add your own thoughts here. What do you think Ellie and Jonas should have done differently in this situation?

_____

_____

_____

_____

Earlier we discussed the issue of giving your stepchild time before you start disciplining. How much time should you give your stepchild before you start? If your stepchild is over age seven, not more than one year. Why? Because this is ample time for them to understand you and know where you're coming from, particularly because in the first stage, you started bonding with your stepchild. Every stepchild is different, but using the guideline of one year allows you time to get to know your stepchild, and how your stepchild reacts and responds to authority figures and also allows you the time to know what works with your stepchild and what does not. If your stepchild is younger than age seven, it's reasonable to feel that your stepchild will adjust to you much more quickly because of their need for structure and routine.

How Your Stepchild Can Benefit

When stepparents think of disciplining their children, generally they feel anxious about it. But here is a way to alleviate that anxiety for you and help you to understand that taking part in disciplining your stepchild can actually benefit them. But please, don't expect your stepchild to thank you for it—at least not until they are adults and a parent themselves!

The age of your stepchild will play a role in disciplining. If your stepchild is under the age of seven, clearly different rules of discipline will apply than if your stepchild is sixteen. For a younger child, parents need to make all of the decisions. But for a teenager who has reached the "age of arguing," you may choose to take a different approach. And here's where the benefit for them comes in. Accept input from your teenaged or young-adult stepchild. You will probably end up negotiating with your stepchild at that age about things anyway, for a couple of reasons. Negotiating prevents continued conflict with teenagers, but it also teaches your teen stepchild a valuable lesson. And that is how to negotiate fairly for things they may want and feel they deserve, as well as learning how to do this with someone other than their bioparent. This negotiation will help prepare your stepchild for relationships with non-related people as adults, both at work and in their social circles.

So, discipline can be a skill that you add to your portfolio as stepparent, but your stepchild can also benefit from discipline—even though they won't realize it at the time! Follow the stages of your Stepfamily Plan, and you will have laid the groundwork for you to safely begin disciplining your stepchild.

Don't underestimate the importance of the support that you will need from your spouse in disciplining. It would be helpful for you to consider additional avenues for support on this topic. Consider these:

1. Write your concerns in your journal and create a history of your experience with disciplining. If you have a second, younger stepchild, this record will help you know what to do the second time around.

2. Seek a stepparent support group in your community to help you on this issue.

3. Start your own stepparent support group with friends and neighbors.

4. Seek professional help from a counselor specializing in stepparent issues.

5. Contact me through my Web site at www.docsuzen.com with questions/comments.

Exercise: Are You Ready to Discipline Your Stepchild?

How will you know when you're ready to participate in discipline? Let's do this exercise.

1. I feel comfortable giving my stepchild advice. ____ Yes ____ No

2. My stepchild likes to spend time with me. ____ Yes ____ No

3. I understand what my spouse expects from me with regards to parenting his or her children. ____ Yes ____ No

4. I can follow through on a decision that I make for my stepchild. ____ Yes ____ No

5. I can say "no" to my stepchild. ____ Yes ____ No

6. I will crumble when my stepchild refuses to obey me. ____ Yes ____ No

7. I can live with my stepchild being upset with me. ____ Yes ____ No

If you answered "yes" to these questions (except number 6), you are ready. If you answered no to *any* of these questions (except for number 6, to which the correct answer is "no"), then you are not yet ready to take on this important task in your job as stepparent. What should you do? Talk with your spouse first and work out a plan to reach the point of saying "yes" to the necessary questions. For example, if you cannot say "no" to your stepchild, understand what is stopping you. It may sound something like:

- I'm afraid my stepchild won't like me.

- I'm afraid my spouse will get mad at me.

- I'm afraid the extended family members will find out and think I'm a mean stepparent.

Whatever the reason might be, identify it, define it, and work out a plan to get past it. For example, if you are afraid your stepchild won't like you, you need to talk with your stepchild about this. As an example, here is Ellie's dialogue with Dane about this issue:

Ellie: Dane, there's something I need to talk with you about.

Dane: Yeah, what did I do wrong?

Ellie: It's nothing you did wrong. It's about me becoming more of a parent to you.

Dane: What? I already have too many parents. Now you, too?

Ellie: (Chuckle. Keep it light) Yeah, it must be tough to have all of these people telling you what to do, huh? We've gotten to know each other in the last year, Dane, and I want to be more involved with your life than I am right now.

Dane: How?

Ellie: Well, I know we have some common interests, and I think our relationship is pretty good right now, but there are some things that I might ask you to do like clean your room or help make dinner sometimes. I wanted you to know ahead of time that I will be doing this, and I wanted us to plan ahead for it.

Dane: Why do we need to do that? I know this is your house too, and I wondered when you'd start in on telling me what to do.

Ellie: I know it must feel like that to you, Dane, but to me, it's a privilege to be your parent, even if that means "telling you what to do" sometimes. I love your father, and I want to be as much a part of your life as he is; at least to the extent that your father thinks is okay. It's fine with your dad for me to take more of a parent role with you. How do you feel about me being another parent?

Dane: Well, if you put it that way, it sounds pretty cool. But give me time to adjust, okay? I don't know you that well, and I might get frustrated if you tell me to do something.

You get the idea. Present this to your stepchild as a special asset to improve your relationship with him, not as an obstacle to it. Your stepchild will respond better, and you will retain a position of respect in your stepfamily to your spouse and your stepchild.

The Other Bioparent's Concerns

The next hurdle that you will need to jump in disciplining your stepchild is how their other parent will feel about you in this role and how you intend to discipline their child. But there is a way for you to confront this issue and plan ahead to prevent a conflict from occurring. How can you accomplish this feat? Simple. Incorporate the issue into your parenting-team topics for discussion.

Step 2: Evaluate Where Your Parenting Team Is

At the end of Stage 1, your parenting team was in place and working. How does your increased role as parent and disciplinarian fit into the parenting team? It is your spouse's responsibility to introduce you to your parenting team members as taking more of an authority role with your stepchild. Why? Because you will have received permission from your spouse to do this, and they need to inform their ex-spouse of this. Your parenting team needs to understand that you are taking on this role, and you need to discipline your stepchild according to the agreement established by your spouse, but you have an added responsibility in discussing this arrangement with your parenting team. Your responsibility is to follow the guidelines set forth by the team. You should absolutely not parent or discipline your stepchild differently than you agreed to with their bioparents! Your job is to follow the rules, just like everyone else on your parenting team.

Define Goals for Your Parenting Team

Let's define goals for Stage 3 in your parenting team.

1. Review any concerns that took place over the first two stages (review your journal!) and to correct any imperfections in your team. Problem solve, be fair, and respect each other.

2. It is essential that the parenting team be a strong support to you in Stage 3 while you tread gently into the disciplinarian role.

3. Your parenting team needs to communicate, communicate, communicate. *Any* concerns about the children need to be discussed, reviewed, and resolved together.

4. Remember the focus of your parenting team is the stepchild—not your feelings about one another or any unresolved problems from the past.

5. Meet as often as needed but at least once per month.

With regards to discipline, the parenting team needs to discuss how discipline is handled in each bioparent home, and that includes how you are proceeding with discipline. But given the level of sensitivity with this issue, what is the best way to discuss discipline with your parenting team?

The parenting team will be comprised of a unique set of members—two bioparents who have been married to each other previously and two new adults newly married to each bioparent (plus anyone else that you feel should be included; sometimes this means grandparents if they parent the stepchild regularly). Each member will bring their own set of concerns to the team. This is not, however, the place to air dislikes about one another—remember goal 4 above. The parenting team is about the stepchild, not the unresolved negative feelings of the adults. When approaching the discipline subject, keep in mind each team member's role. A bioparent may be much more passionate about this issue than you, particularly the ex-spouse if they sense that you might in any way be unintentionally harming their child through disciplining them. Try to be supportive and nondefensive with the ex-spouse in your parenting team. They may be feeling guilty about the divorce, and could feel that their child requires additional nurturing. You may see the stepchild differently. It's okay to see things differently as long as you are diplomatic if you do feel the ex-spouse may be wrong. Approach this gently, looking to your spouse for support.

Ross and Jena's Story

Jena and Ross had planned carefully for their biological children when they knew they were going to become a stepfamily. Both Jena and

Ross knew that it would important that the children felt secure and received consistent guidance and direction from all the parents in all of the households involved. But what would be the best way to ensure this for the children?

Jena and Ross created their parenting team in the first stage with the sole goal of providing consistent parenting for the children. Their parenting team moved along fine the first few months and although some arguments took place, they were able to focus on the children and their needs. The ex-spouses were in full support of the parenting-team concepts, and their new spouses felt the benefits of this parenting consistency as well. In the third stage, Ross and Jena expected their team to become even stronger and more supportive of one another. And this happened—until Ross stated that Jena would be taking more of a disciplinary role with his children. Ross' ex-wife had a concern with this, and although Jena understood, she felt Ross' ex-wife needed to understand how difficult stepparenting would be if Jena did not begin to be the other parent in the stepfamily. Reacting to past feelings of inadequacy around his ex-wife, Ross started withdrawing his support of Jena in the parenting role. Of course, Jena sensed this, and their relationship suffered because of Jena not feeling Ross supported her in the issue. As a result, Jena and Ross, who had carefully implemented the parenting team, were now experiencing friction because of it!

What did Ross and Jena do? First of all, it was up to Ross to renew his support for Jena and to express this at the next parenting-team meeting. Ross knew that he was reacting to old "baggage" and that this wasn't appropriate, particularly in his new stepfamily and new intimate relationship with Jena. Ross reiterated at the next parenting-team meeting that he truly did support Jena in taking more of a parenting and authority role with the children, and he proceeded to explain to his ex-wife the reasons that *she* also needed to be supportive of Jena in this role—for the children.

It is so easy for bioparents and stepparents to fall back into the old roles they played in their previous relationship, and particularly into behaviors that were familiar but perhaps not the most productive or effective. As a stepparent, you need to be as aware of this potential stumbling block, as does your spouse. Any old behaviors that were destructive in your previous relationships need to be examined and probably changed or modified so that you don't fall back into old patterns that were destructive in your relationships. Jena and Ross were successful in their third stage, and Jena received the support from her parenting team that she needed.

Keep Communicating!

Let's talk about communication in your parenting team. Communication is so important in our society today, and it affects every part of our lives—socially, in our stepfamily, or in the workplace. Communication is the key to accomplishing goals, particularly the goals in your parenting team. In Stage 3, your parenting team will need to communicate even more than before. Why? Because in the first two stages you became organized as a team and struggled to overcome your negative feelings about one another. In Stage 3, the real work begins. That means the parenting team needs to focus on the children and what is best for them from each of the parents.

You and your parenting-team members need to be mentors to the children and you need to visibly represent yourselves as a cohesive group—as members that work together toward a goal. This is one of the greatest gifts that you and your parenting team could give your children, to see their parents, the people they look up to the most, working together with their new spouses and their ex-spouses. Wow—think of how powerful that could be for your children. You will be teaching them how to maintain relationships even through conflict. Your stepchildren will benefit from your parenting team in many ways, but this is one of the greatest achievements for you and your team members. And how can you achieve this? By communicating effectively in your parenting team. Each member has the right to contribute to the team. Remember to limit the time of the meeting to prevent any one member from dominating the meeting or to prevent any one member from getting off on a tangent that has little to do with the parenting-team focus.

Complete the summary of Stage 3 immediately after reading the chapter. The information will be fresh in your mind. Then when you review your Stepfamily Plan at the specified timelines, you will update the summary information to determine how your stepfamily has made progress in the area of discipline and its challenges.

Quick Stage 3 Summary

Step I: Taking the Discipline Challenge

How did your stepfamily do? Did you make an attempt to take more authority? Check one.

___ Good job ___ Need some improvement ___ I need more help with this!

Do you feel you have learned a correct and effective way to discipline?
____ Yes ____ No, I still need work on this

Where are you in disciplining? Circle one.

1. I don't feel comfortable with this

2. I'm leaving it up to my partner

3. I am sharing this with my partner

4. I am doing most of the discipline now

Other feelings you have about discipline:

_____

_____

_____

What did you learn about yourself because of the discipline issue?

_____

_____

_____

What did you learn about your stepchild?

_____

_____

_____

Did you receive support in the discipline issue from your spouse?
____ Yes ____ No

If not, you need to seek professional help, particularly if you plan to share in the parenting and disciplining of your child. It is your spouse's job to support you in this.

Are you continuing to write in your journal? ____ Yes ____ No

If not, it's not too late to start writing in your journal regularly. Please write an entry into your journal today at the end of this chapter!

Step 2: Evaluate Where Your Parenting Team Is

How is the communication in your parenting team? Check one.

____ Nonexistent

____ Our goal is to keep this to a minimum

____ Started poorly, but improving now

____ Wonderful, we really enjoy working together

I would like to see my parenting team work harder at:

_____

_____

_____

_____

What have you learned about yourself in the parenting team? What have you learned about your spouse?

_____

_____

_____

What have you learned about your stepchild?

_____

_____

_____

What have you learned about your parenting-team members?

_____

_____

_____

_____

Excellent job stepparent. Now let's take a look at the extended family member issues that will affect your stepfamily.

My Stepfamily Journal

Chapter 8

Stage 4: Navigate the Extended Family Circuit

A stepparent once told me that she was intimidated by her extended family members. When I asked why, she realized that it was their reaction to her that concerned her the most. This stepparent had made a realization that day; until then, she hadn't been certain about what bothered her about her stepfamily's extended family network. The point is you need to define *exactly* what the issue might be that makes you uncomfortable with your extended family so that you can take steps to fix it.

Step 1: How Do You Feel About Your Stepfamily's Extended Family?

First, let's look at why we need to examine this issue. Extended family members are very important to your stepfamily. Why? As we discussed earlier, it's the extended family members who represent your spouse and stepchild's histories. Extended family are invaluable to the development of your stepfamily because your spouse and stepchild will integrate their extended family members into the stepfamily. So you will be involved with this group, and you will have interactions with them. Sometimes, however, the extended family can seem threatening or intimidating to stepparents. Why? Because you may not realize that this extended group of people are evaluating you in your new role as stepparent and that's important because they may influence your spouse and stepchild. How do we handle this? First, let's identify who the extended stepfamily members are, and then develop a plan to build relationships with them.

- Grandparents—the stepchild's maternal and paternal grandparents

- Aunts and uncles—these folks will be your spouse's siblings and your stepchild's other parent's siblings

- Cousins—your stepchild's cousins whose parents are your spouse's siblings and your husband's ex-spouse's siblings

- Close friends of the previous family may be considered here also

- Extended family members include anybody from the previous family that will affect your stepfamily directly or indirectly

- Add specific extended family members in *your* stepfamily not included here:

_____

_____

_____

There are several issues that you will probably struggle with in your stepfamily with regards to extended family members. These issues include:

- What should your stepchild call your extended family members?

- What relationship should you have with your stepfamily's extended family?

- Should their extended family be a part of your extended family?

- What type of boundaries should be in place?

List your questions about your extended family members:

_____

_____

_____

What's Good about Their Extended Family?

Now let's look at the positive aspects of including the extended family. Your stepchild's extended family members can greatly contribute to your role as stepparent. How? They are an additional support to your stepfamily toward building a strong, cohesive stepfamily from the outside. What does "from the outside" mean? Your job is to help build a strong internal stepfamily structure, but your extended family can help you build a strong stepfamily with their more objective point of view. Your extended family members will see that you are an important part of their family's life—that you are an asset to the stepchild and their bioparent. By showing this to your extended family members, you have helped them understand your desire to provide a stable and happy family life for your spouse and your stepchild. Is it politics? Yeah, sure it is. Is it fair? Not necessarily, but think of it as a deposit in your future investment—anybody investing in your future needs to be shown that the investment is solid. You need to demonstrate to your new extended family that you're worth investing in for the future.

Why is this so important to your Stepfamily Plan? The biggest reason is that stepfamilies can fail because of extended family pressures. Oftentimes these pressures occur because the extended family may not like you or their perception of you. Extended family can sometimes influence spouses and stepchildren. It's your job to be sure that the extended family members get to know you as a person and that they understand your motives toward your new stepfamily.

Step 2: Looking at *Your* Extended Family Members

There is also the question of your family members. We need to cover issues that your stepchild will need to know about these folks, including what your stepchild should call them.

Nomenclature

What should your stepchild call your extended family members? This question comes up frequently in stepfamilies because the stepchild is expected to have a relationship with your extended family, which is often uncomfortable because they don't know your family members very well. First, you need to make a decision about the level of involvement you expect your stepchild to have with your extended family (based on your family's comfort level too, of course). If you want your stepchild to have a relationship with your family, talk with your spouse about it. Plan ahead for these relationships. Don't just expect your stepchild to know what to do. Here's your chance to be proactive and take a leading role as stepparent.

Here are some guidelines to help you create a plan to integrate your two families.

- Don't pressure your stepchild to have a relationship with your extended family.

- Talk with your stepchild about how you'd like the relationship to work first to explain the process of integrating two families.

- Tell them what you expect from them but be understanding of their position.

- Ask them to call your parents Grandma and Grandpa (if that's what you want).

- Tell your stepchild why this is important to you.

- Your stepchild may find this difficult—help them do it. The last thing you should do is get upset with your stepchild if they *don't* want to do this or if they don't do it exactly right the first couple of times.

- Understand that your stepchild already has a couple of sets of grandparents, and they may feel uncomfortable with calling another, unfamiliar couple what they call their grandparents, whom they are close to. It's okay if your stepchild doesn't want to call your parents Grandma and Grandpa. They have another family already in place, and they will want to remain loyal to their own extended family. That's normal. Don't make this a battle.

- Be patient. These are incredibly important requests, but the rewards are worth waiting for.

- The same idea applies to your aunts and uncles. Stepchildren will likely be confused by all of the additional extended family members that you will bring to the stepfamily. They should be expected to treat your family members with kindness and respect, but you really shouldn't expect your stepchild to know each by name or how they are related to you. Over time, your stepchild may show an interest in your extended family, but don't expect that to happen right away—stepchildren generally will not meet your expectations on this. Don't be disappointed. Allow your stepchild to adjust to your extended family in their own time.

There is the issue of the age of your stepchild. For example, if your stepchild is under the age of seven, it's acceptable to introduce your parents as grandparents to your stepchild, and they likely will call them by that endearing term. I encourage you, however, to discuss this with your spouse first. Your spouse may not want this, and it is your spouse's decision that will take priority for their child. If your stepchild is in their teens and older, allow them the time to make the adjustment in their own way. Of course, the rule of respect and kindness applies to all ages. But a teen or older stepchild will likely resist your efforts if they feel pushed or forced to call your parents Grandma and Grandpa when they really don't recognize the relationship in that way. It's perfectly acceptable for your teen or young-adult stepchild to address them as Mr., Mrs., or by their first names.

Case History: Briggs and Gina

Gina and Briggs were married for a short time when the extended family member issue came to the surface. Gina wanted Briggs' daughters, Liz and Arizona, twelve and thirteen years old, to call her parents Grandma and Grandpa. She had felt that once they were married, that her parents would be hurt if Liz and Arizona didn't call them Grandma and Grandpa. Gina went ahead and told Liz and Arizona what she wanted. Promptly, Liz and Arizona, feeling uncomfortable with the request, told their dad.

Briggs was upset. First of all, Gina had not talked with Briggs first, and secondly, he felt Liz and Arizona had been through enough with the divorce, and didn't need to be pressured to do something they weren't comfortable with. Once Briggs knew what Gina had done, he confronted her, and the conflict began. Gina felt betrayed by Briggs because he supported his children and not her on this, and Gina also felt that Briggs didn't understand what she needed in the situation.

Where did the conflict occur with Gina and Briggs? Not with the stepchildren, but between Gina and Briggs. This was problematic because a well-intended desire on Gina's part became a conflict between the two people who needed to be understanding of each other the most. But what would be the best way to resolve this? Briggs has a point, but Gina as the stepparent has a right to want to include her parents in her new stepfamily.

In this situation, Gina and Briggs compromised. Instead of requiring Liz and Arizona to call Gina's parents Grandma and Grandpa, they talked with Liz and Arizona about what happened with the situation. They explained why the issue was important to Gina, and once Liz and Arizona knew this, they understood. But the girls still felt uncomfortable about what to call Gina's parents. Briggs and Gina, still wanting to be in control of this issue, gave Liz and Arizona choices on what to call Gina's parents—by their first names or by Mr. and Mrs. This turned into a win-win situation. The girls no longer felt uncomfortable, Briggs felt reassured that Gina was not unnecessarily pressuring his children, and Gina's feelings were shared with her stepchildren so they understood her position better. Everybody won.

Step 3: Your Relationship with Their Extended Family

This has always been and remains a mystery with most stepfamilies. Why? Because navigating this network of people who are evaluating your stepparent abilities becomes a task you may want to withdraw from altogether! You may feel inadequate and insecure around this group of people. Why? Because it can be overwhelming to meet the family members who know the history of your spouse and stepchild's previous family. Sometimes this can be threatening to a stepparent and it may make you feel uncomfortable. If this is happening to you, here is what you can do about it.

First, you need to get to know each extended family member as an individual. It's important that you develop a relationship with each member of your spouse and stepchild's extended family, on any level. You can be close to the extended family members, or you can choose to stay at a distance. Either way, the key is to make a connection with extended family members so that they come to know you as an individual—not as an appendage of your spouse and stepchild. If they don't know you as an individual, they may make assumptions about you and your ability to stepparent or function in this stepfamily. This could be potentially harmful to your stepfamily, so you want to prevent that.

Here is an example of a dialogue that you can begin with an extended family member. In this example, you are talking with your stepchild's Aunt Loralie, who is also your spouse's ex-sister-in-law.

You: Loralie, I know that you knew Jacie (your spouse's ex-wife), before Jack and I were married.

Loralie: Yes, and it's a little awkward to be talking with you.

You: Well, I can understand that, Loralie. I'm feeling uncomfortable myself.

Loralie: Jacie may be at these family get-togethers sometimes, and I don't want to betray her by talking with you.

You: I understand that, too, but when I married Jack, I knew I couldn't replace Jacie in the family—and it's not my intention to do that. But I was hoping that we could get to know each other better. Would that be all right with you Loralie?

Loralie: Well, I don't know. Jacie might feel hurt. You know, it wasn't her fault that Jack left.

You: I don't want to hurt Jacie, but I would like us to know each other just a little better so that family gatherings can be less stressful for the kids and the adults.

Loralie: You're right, and I want to be fair to you, too. I'll talk with Jacie and maybe we can all figure out a way to reach a family balance.

You: Thanks for understanding, Loralie.

What just happened here? You had a conversation with an extended family member from the previous family. It was a bit uncomfortable at first, but relatively nonthreatening and you've taken a first step in positioning yourself in the extended family. This is a step-by-step process, and it's important that you take it slowly. Don't push too hard to be included. Your spouse and stepchild's extended family members need time to accept you, particularly if the divorce was difficult and family members chose sides. You need to present yourself as an individual, independent of your spouse. They need to get to know *you*—the caring and nurturing new member of this family that clearly loves their family members, your spouse, and/or your stepchild. Once they feel assured that you are an asset to the family, you have done your job in strengthening your stepfamily and in securing a solid position for yourself in this new extended family network.

Setting Boundaries with Extended Family Members

Boundaries are particularly important in stepfamilies. Why? Because of the complicated relationships that exist not only between the stepparent and stepchild, but also what potentially could complicate things for your stepfamily with members of the previous extended family. Your stepfamily will have issues of its own and does not need to be complicated by extended family members who may resent you because of what happened in your spouse's last marriage. Boundaries need to be in place with your stepchild's extended family members to prevent any unnecessary problems. Those boundaries should include the following:

- Be sure you make your stepfamily members a priority.

- Don't get into arguments with your stepchild's extended family members about what may or may not have happened in their previous family.

- Do not allow your stepchild's extended family members to come between you and your spouse or you and your stepchild.

Why is this information helpful? Because it's important that you stay focused on your stepfamily and put all of your energy into building a strong and healthy future for all of you together.

Planning for These Relationships

Now, let's look at building a plan to create these relationships that will need to be long-term. The first step in this plan can be acknowledging and accepting the importance that your stepfamily's extended family has. The most important quality that extended family members bring to your stepfamily is the history that they share with your stepfamily. You must not underestimate this connection, and you must not ignore it. The best way to accept the extended family into your stepfamily is with kindness and an open mind.

Your Three Most Important Goals

The three most important goals in working to incorporate extended families into your Stepfamily Plan should be:

1. To be supportive of your stepfamily,

2. To enhance your stepfamily by being a resource for strength, and

3. To provide a history for your stepfamily.

How do you achieve these goals? First, you must appreciate the role your extended family members play in your stepfamily.

- Be understanding that it's a transition for them to accept and get to know you.

- If you experience conflict with an extended family member because they may resent you as the new member, start a dialogue, invite them to get to know you, and most importantly, don't give up. This will take time.

- Be empathetic to their position. Help them to understand who you are as an individual.

Secondly, create your relationship with extended family members.

- Present yourself as an asset to them.

- Be the nurturing and understanding stepparent they need you to be.

- Don't resent your new extended family members because of their ties with the ex-spouse.

- You need to be the adult and begin to encourage mending any fences that have been knocked down in the past.

Thirdly, maintain your relationship with extended family—just when you thought your job was done by simply building these relationships! Sorry, but the work will continue with this one.

- Remember, you don't need to be best friends with extended family members, but your relationship with them should be special and important to you.

- Keep these relationships strong. The best way to do this is to have a stable and well-adjusted stepfamily.

- Be good to your extended family members. You are a member of their club now and hold all of the rights to this membership. Honor the rules and abide by them, but remember that you can also influence the rules and begin to create your own.

Case History: Connor and Ariel

Ariel and Connor married after a short time together and Ariel brought her child, Annie, into the family. Connor was surprised at Annie's extended family member's reaction to him after he and Ariel married. Annie's maternal grandparents, aunts, and uncles were distant, and, as Connor described, "standoffish" to him. Connor had not felt this prior to their marriage, but then Connor had only limited contact with Annie's other family prior to marrying Ariel.

Connor had tried to talk with the grandparents and aunts and uncles at Annie's graduation party, but he quickly gave up because he felt there was no point. After all, these were Annie's family members, not his. Why would he need to interact with them in the future?

Connor quickly learned, however, that he would be having more to do with them than he'd thought. Ariel's family gathered often, particularly to celebrate Annie's achievements such as school events and birthdays. And then there were the holiday and summer gatherings. Ariel, of course, invited Annie's other family to these get togethers, too.

Connor knew he needed to do better with these family members but he wasn't sure how to proceed. I asked Connor to try working on one family member at a time. Connor then tried several approaches such as calling and inviting them for a conversation in a neutral place such as a coffee shop or a diner where they could get to know each other as individuals.

Talking with family members one-on-one worked effectively for Connor because he was able to get to know each family member as an individual and try to understand their specific feelings. Talking this way also helped Connor reduce his anxiety about facing the entire group of family all at once because at the next family gathering, Connor knew several family members individually and felt comfortable approaching them in conversation.

What Is Their Responsibility?

As the stepparent, you certainly have the decision-making ability to take control of some issues in your stepfamily. This is what being proactive in your stepfamily is all about, and is the basis for this Stepfamily Plan that you are creating through reading and participating in this book. You have the power to change or influence many issues in your role as stepparent, plus you have responsibilities in your job as a stepparent. Well, other members of your stepfamily, even extended family members have several responsibilities of their own.

1. They have a responsibility to have an open mind with stepparents. It's natural to have preconceived notions about people, and it's also reasonable to expect that their first impression of you may shape their feelings about you entirely. You may be doing the same things with them!

2. Extended family members have a responsibility in giving you a chance.

3. Extended family members owe it to their relative, the stepchild, to give her new stepfamily every opportunity to be successful and fulfilling.

Will I Ever Be a Part of This Family?

What happens if you've done everything that you can and still feel as though there is little cooperation from everybody else? Let's hope you will not have to deal with this, but if you do, the best advice is for you to develop effective coping skills to help you through the rough spots.

What are some coping skills that you'd do well to acquire to reach your goal of decreasing the conflict while resolving past conflict?

• In the short term, understand the causes of the conflict.

• Once you know the cause, you can begin to problem solve it.

• Identify if you are contributing to any conflict. How? Analyze your own behavior and actions. Only you can change how you approach people.

A second goal should be to increase the number of positive family interactions. How?

- Plan ahead for the family event that is coming up. Role play with your spouse by acting out an interaction with a family member whom you feel you may conflict with. Practice your responses; you'll be surprised at how much easier interactions become with practice.

- Lastly, look to your spouse for support. It is the bioparent's job to help you fit in, and if there is conflict you feel cannot be worked out, ask your spouse to help.

Now, complete the following summary based on the chapter information. Remember to be genuine in your answers so that you have an honest and solid foundation of information to begin with and to review toward modification and progress later.

Quick Stage 4 Summary

Step 1: How Do You Really Feel about Your Stepfamily's Extended Family Members?

Check one.

_____ They are impossible

_____ Difficult group, but I think I am making headway

_____ They are surprisingly wonderful to me, given the circumstances

What is the most positive attribute about your stepfamily's extended family?

_____ They appear to be understanding of the past

_____ They are all quite pleasant

_____ They are willing to accept me

Add your own:

_____

_____

Step 2: Planning for Their Involvement in Your Family

_____ I will have this plan completed by _____

_____ I'm waiting on this because my stepchild doesn't seem to like me very much right now

_____ I plan to talk to my stepchild about this on _____

_____ My stepchild and I will plan this together

Step 3: Your Relationship with Their Extended Family

What is your goal for your level of involvement?

_____ Very little contact

_____ I plan to do the best I can to feel included in this extended family

_____ I will be assertive and make the first move

_____ I want them to feel comfortable with our stepfamily, so I will personally invite them to celebrations at our home

Determine which extended family member might be approachable.

_____ My stepchild's maternal grandparents

_____ My stepchild's aunt

_____ My stepchild's uncle

Identify the person in your situation whom you can approach:

_____

I will talk to this person on (date)

_____

Great job. Now, do your journaling about your thoughts and feelings on extended family. Try to be as detailed as possible. Details will help you later on as you modify and evaluate your stepfamily's progress. This was a tough chapter, so give yourself a pat on the back. You are doing just fine.

Once your journaling is complete, grab that cup of cappuccino, and let's give your marriage some extra special attention to ensure its survival.

My Stepfamily Journal

Chapter 9

Stage 5: Will My Marriage Survive?

Stepfamily issues can get so involved that the adults in the stepfamily tend to forget to pay attention to their marriage, the single most important cornerstone in the stepfamily of today. Your marriage is primary, and you need to pay lots of attention to it! You need to treat your marriage as a special, fragile piece of china. Treat it gently, admire it when you look at it, keep it polished and looking like new.

Step 1: Keeping Your Marriage Healthy

Remember when you checked your emotional barometer on alienation? Well, in Stage 5, you need to check your emotional barometer for your marriage. Step 1 is the only step in this chapter because it is so important. It is essential in a stepfamily that you keep your marriage at the top of your priority list of things you must be successful at. Your marriage is vitally important to the success of your stepfamily, and it must remain at the core of your stepfamily's solidarity. In this chapter, we will continue to discuss your marriage and focus specifically on what you can do for your marriage as part of a stepfamily and how a marriage within a stepfamily differs from a marriage in a traditional family environment. Knowing this difference will give you the ability to plan ahead for the stability of your marriage and allow you to avoid many pitfalls that stepparents face unexpectedly.

In Stage 5, you need to check how you are feeling about your marriage. Is your marriage meeting your needs? Is your marriage what you thought it would be? Is it still your priority? If not, make it your priority. Your marriage will *always* need to be the priority. Remember that. It's not only important how you feel your marriage is doing but equally important is how your spouse is feeling about your marriage. Is your spouse happy? Is the marriage satisfying to both of you?

Exercise: Key Areas to Review in Your Marriage

You and your spouse should each complete this exercise. Some of this information may be sensitive and difficult for you, but please be honest and specific. The results will be a valuable tool for both of you in analyzing areas in your marriage that might need immediate and significant attention to improve.

Evaluate each of the following areas:

Do you frequently or continually argue with your spouse?
_____ Yes _____ No

Do you lack good communication with your spouse?
_____ Yes _____ No

Is there a pattern of blaming each other for the conflicts in the stepfamily?
_____ Yes _____ No

Is one or both of you avoiding one another?
_____ Yes _____ No

Do you or your spouse spend excessive time at work or recreation to be away from the house?
_____ Yes _____ No

Do you trust one another?
_____ Yes _____ No

How deep is your love for one another? Describe this in one sentence.

_____

_____

Has anything changed in your marriage? If so, what?

_____

_____

What is the one best thing about your marriage?

_____

_____

What is one thing you would like changed about your marriage?

_____

_____

Be sure to keep a check on your marriage frequently throughout Stage 5. The more involved you become in your stepfamily, the easier it is to lose sight of your intimate relationship and the easier it is to blame the person you love the most when things go wrong. It's strange, but true.

Give Your Marriage a Gift

If any of the above is a concern in your marriage, what should you do? One of the best gifts you can give your marriage is to develop the ability to handle conflicts in a mature, controlled, nonaggressive yet resolution-focused way. What does this mean? The adults in a stepfamily need to work even harder at making the marriage work. How? By making the effort to self-examine and make improvements in how you act and react to conflicts in relationships. Take a minute to review how you argued in your last relationship. If it didn't work for you then, it probably won't work for you in your new relationship. The same advice applies to your new spouse. Changing partners isn't always the answer to a successful marriage. But changing you, particularly the way you react, can be the key to greater success this time around.

Step 2: How Do You Handle Conflict?

Conflicts and disagreements can and will occur even in the best of relationships. So the goal is not to eliminate conflicts, because that might be impossible. Rather, your aim is to learn how to act and react better to the conflicts that will occur. Here comes that planning thing again. If you can plan how you will react to conflicts, you may not reduce the number of conflicts (however there is a good chance that will happen), but you *can* reduce the degree of anger, hostility, disappointment, and resentment that can occur. You will create an environment in this marriage that will be more comfortable, and you will feel better about yourself particularly if you handle disagreements maturely and in a controlled manner. You will also teach your stepchild how to do the same, simply by modeling this behavior. Remember, your stepchild is watching you, both when you are happy and when you might be angry. They will mimic your behavior and your actions. Show them how to handle relationships maturely and calmly. Learning how to argue or to negotiate your position is a skill that will reward you again and again, not only in your stepfamily but in other areas in your life as well.

What can you do to learn how to react less defensively, act more appropriately, and handle conflict more diplomatically?

Exercise: Working on Conflict

First, identify the causes for any present conflicts in your marriage.

How do conflicts/disagreements start in your house?

_____

_____

_____

Have your spouse answer this question, too.

_____

_____

_____

You and your spouse should point out to each other the changes you feel the other needs to make.

I feel my spouse needs to make changes in the area of:

_____

_____

Discuss the emotions you feel during a conflict such as denial, guilt, anger, embarrassment, fear or loneliness with your spouse

Identify your role in the conflicts

Do you become angry immediately and then the argument goes downhill from there? _____ Yes _____ No

Do you avoid taking responsibility when you're wrong? _____ Yes   No

Do you initiate the conflict? _____ Yes _____ No

What can you change?

- Increase the time you enjoy spending together.

- If you argue things to death simply to win an argument, then stop.

- Learn to *really* listen to what your spouse is saying. Often one member of the relationship is apologizing and is done arguing and the other hasn't even realized it.

- Make a list of changes you need to make to improve how you react and respond to conflict.

- Add your own: _____

I continually receive inquiries from stepparents who struggle with their marriage—generally as the result of problems due to the stepfamily pressures. Why do we tend to want to give up on our marriage when things are going wrong in the stepfamily? Lots of reasons.

- First, the problems in stepfamilies drain your energy. You spend so much time worrying about trying to fix the stepfamily problems that it becomes overwhelming, and there is little energy left for the marriage.

- Secondly, you become disappointed with your spouse because you feel they aren't doing what you need them to do. Sadly, this disappointment equates to a disappointing marriage, and you may start to think the marriage was a mistake.

- Thirdly, you start to feel like an outsider all over again when conflicts occur in the stepfamily, and you begin to feel that you will never really be a part of this stepfamily and become alienated from the marriage as a result. Problems in stepfamilies are a common theme in second marriages breaking up today. Let's discuss how your marriage can make it through your stepfamily!

What You Can Do for Your Marriage

As a stepparent, you know the challenges of a first marriage, and here you are in a subsequent marriage, struggling not only to keep the stepfamily stable but also wanting your new marriage to work. How do you juggle all of this? How can a stepfamily remain stable if the marriage doesn't, and vice versa? Can a marriage survive in a stepfamily?

Well, simply put, if your marriage isn't nurtured and cared for, it's likely your stepfamily will not survive either. Sounds grim, yes. But can the marriage and stepfamily not only survive, but thrive as well? You bet it can, and in this chapter, you will learn how to not only manage them both, but you will also learn techniques to build a happy marriage.

The Single Most Important Issue

What is the single most important issue in your marriage to a bioparent? That's an easy one. Being in love with that bioparent. Now, what is the second most important issue? Accepting their children. But being in love with your spouse is an asset in traditional as well as stepfamilies. So, why shouldn't that be enough for both types of families? Well, as a stepparent, you will understand this very well. In a stepfamily, being in love with your spouse isn't enough—you must also accept your spouse's children because they are part of the marriage, too; not in an intimate way, but certainly as part of the foundation, structure, and dynamic of your stepfamily. Stepfamilies are instant families. There is little time for you and your spouse to be alone without the presence of the children. And, yes, some traditional families have children before or soon after they are married. The only difference in a stepfamily is that you and the stepchildren are not unconditionally accepting of one another. There is a great deal of work and effort on your part to accept the stepchild at all. As a result, your marriage requires more effort and understanding than if it were just you, your spouse, and your own *biological* children.

There is a huge difference with stepchildren—there are conditions placed upon the relationship between a stepchild and a stepparent. It can be similar to living with roommates or strangers. You are highly conscious of the presence of your stepchildren in the house. You may even be preoccupied with them while you are at work or at a social function, wondering how your stepchild is doing or how he or she is feeling about you. There are conditions that have to be met in this relationship. You need to work through accepting this relationship completely and fully so that not only your stepfamily can survive, but so your marriage can survive as well.

It sounds like lots of the responsibility for the marriage is placed on you, right? Well, in fact that is often what takes place in stepfamilies. Why? It's generally the stepparent who is most concerned with the realities of the stepfamily, and it's often the stepparent who must prove themselves. The stepparent must be the one who works at accepting the daily life of the stepfamily, which means living with someone else's children. And, it's usually the stepparent who tends to be most concerned with the survival of the stepfamily and the marriage. Why? Because the stepparent feels responsible if the stepfamily is failing and as a result, they feel the responsibility if the marriage is also failing. Is this fair? No. Does it occur? Yes, and all too often.

As a stepparent, you may feel that the marriage is failing because your relationship with your stepchild isn't the greatest. Or you feel guilty because of the way you handle things in the stepfamily—maybe you become too angry or maybe you're too passive. Perhaps you think that the marriage isn't going to work out because of your behavior. Or you feel that the bioparent isn't doing what he needs to do, but you're not sure if you are expecting too much. You may even suspect that the failure of your marriage is your fault because you can't do this stepfamily thing. If you are feeling this way, first, please do not feel alone. Many stepparents struggle with these issues and many stepparents feel then that marrying a person with children is a mistake. At that point, much ground has been lost and much more work is required on the part of both adults to maintain the marriage. The key is to not let it get to this point in the first place. The more you monitor your marriage early on and keep things working, the less risk you will take in losing precious time in having to save your marriage later on.

Warning Signs of Marriage Failure in a Stepfamily

What signs should you be keeping your eyes out for?

- You withdraw from the stepfamily and start to isolate from your stepfamily members.

- Your stepchild and bioparent spend much more time together than you and your spouse do.

- You have feelings that your marriage was a mistake and you start telling yourself this.

- Your communication with stepfamily members decreases.

- Your frustration level with your spouse increases significantly.

- You don't feel "in love."

- You feel as though you will never fit in this stepfamily.

- You are unable to envision this stepfamily working.

- You feel you are doing all of the work in the stepfamily and the marriage.

- You feel that you are the failure and that the stepfamily not working is all your fault.

- You resent your stepchild.

Let's do a barometer check on your marriage to a bioparent. Where do you stand on each of these above issues? If two or more of the above are occurring in your marriage right now, you may be at risk for marriage failure. What should you do? Talk with your spouse first. Share the issues you are feeling and use the above list as your guide. Find out how your spouse is feeling on these issues. If you can work out a plan for resolving these problems together, then create that plan as a partnership. Write the plan down. Tape it to your bathroom mirror or some other visible place. Keep working at the plan daily to help save your marriage. Make this commitment work.

Secondly, you may want to find a stepparent or stepfamily support group. If your spouse is supportive, you could both join a stepfamily support group. You may be surprised at the similarity in the issues that you all face, and you will find support in a safe place to express your concerns.

Finally, if you require more intensive help, seek counseling. It is well worth the investment in your marriage and the rest of your life.

Ensure Your Marriage Is Working

What can you do to ensure your marriage is working?

- The first thing you need to do is identify why you married your spouse in the first place. You need to write this in your journal (writing an abbreviated version below), because you may need to remind yourself of this at particularly difficult moments during your marriage. Everyone has a special reason for marrying their spouse. It will be imperative that you keep this reason alive and special in a marriage within a stepfamily.

What is the one special reason that you married your spouse?

_____ _____

_____ _____

_____ _____

The second thing you need is to be sure you and your spouse are taking time for one another. This is absolutely essential in a stepfamily. Why? Because you and your spouse need time alone together. You will need time away from your stepchildren to spend only with your spouse. As the bioparent, your spouse must understand this.

How much time do you spend alone with your spouse?

_____ Not enough

_____ Enough but I'd still like more

_____ Too much—we're okay on this issue

This is important because if you don't have quality time with your spouse, you may begin to resent her. This may lead to stress in the marriage and eventual warning signs of marriage failure.

The third thing to remember is to make your spouse the most special person in your life—every day. You must laugh often, hold hands and show affection toward one another, and say kind words to each other daily. Take the initiative even if your spouse doesn't; acts of kindness and affection are contagious. You start, and your spouse will respond positively and favorably.

When was the last time you spoke a kind word to your spouse?

_____

What did you do/say?

_____

Whatever you do today, take the time to be kind to your spouse.

Also make a point to show kindness to your stepchild. This is one of the best ways to ensure that your marriage is working. Why? Because if you show your spouse that you care for their child, your spouse will feel secure about the marriage and, in turn, feel secure about you.

When were you last kind to your stepchild?

_____

What did you say?

_____

Make your marriage the number-one priority in your life. Put all other stressors and concerns in your life in second place. Your marriage and your spouse are the most important responsibilities in your life in a stepfamily. You need to make working at your marriage your job. By the way, your spouse needs to do that, too.

Consider Your Spouse's Perspective

What is the bioparent's perspective on the marriage when the stepfamily isn't going well? It's only fair to include the bioparent's viewpoint here. It allows you to understand what your spouse might be thinking but is unable to verbalize.

Probably the first thing the bioparent thinks is that it's the stepparent's fault. This comes from two points of view. First, the bioparent will think that their kids can do no wrong and will truly believe this. The feeling comes from the bioparent's belief that their child is fragile and their guilt feelings from the divorce. Add to these the fact that they have introduced someone new to the family who is putting stress on their child, whom they assume is already as stressed out as much as the bioparent is.

The second reason for placing the blame on the stepparent is that the stepparent is older and should be the adult and able to head off these problems so as to avoid any conflict. The bioparent makes this assumption, however, without allowing for the stepparent's lack of knowledge about the stepchild or the family dynamics that already exist.

Now, the bioparent is questioning whether or not they should have allowed this outsider into their family. Yes, things like separation and divorce flash before the bioparent's eyes. They start questioning immediately why they ever did this to their kids. Did they want companionship, an intimate relationship, financial stability, or help raising the family? Whatever the reason, they begin analyzing why they allowed this outsider into their intimate family circle. They also feel that the relationship with the child, even if distant, carries more weight than the relationship with their new spouse. The structure of the marriage becomes weak, at best.

On rare occasions, the bioparent sides with the stepparent and sees the problem for what it is. This makes solving the problem easier, but because of the bioparent's guilt, it rarely happens. Could this process happen in reverse? Certainly, but then the bioparent is siding with the stepparent and the stepchild is forced to change their procedure from what they have always known in the past as the accepted way of acting inside the natural family. This doesn't work for the bioparent. Often, it is only a matter of time before the bioparent starts thinking that this relationship with the stepparent isn't going to work. The longer the conflict between the members of the stepfamily go on, the stronger the thoughts of separation become. This places stress on the bioparent and that trickles down to every member of the stepfamily. It's not long before members of the stepfamily no longer see the big picture but focus only on the incidents that have caused the hurt and annoyance.

In summary, the most important piece of information from this chapter for you is the importance of the bioparent's perspective in the stepfamily. When I speak about this topic, I often refer to the bioparent as the "glue." Why? Because the bioparent is the key person linking the other relationships. Many conflicts that occur in the stepfamily will rely on the bioparent's conflict-resolution skills and the strength of your bioparent will help tremendously toward the strength of your stepfamily. By showing your spouse that you are helping to resolve conflicts in the stepfamily, you are strengthening the glue that holds your stepfamily together.

Quick Stage 5 Summary

Step 1: Keeping Your Marriage Healthy

Are you happy with your marriage? ____ Yes ____ No

What is the greatest asset in your marriage?

____ Our love for each other

____ Our ability to solve problems

____ Our parenting skills

____ We make each other laugh

____ We like Italian food

Add your own:

_____

_____

Did you identify the causes for any conflict in your marriage?
____ Yes ____ No

What is the source of conflict?

_____

Did you identify *your* role in the conflicts? ____ Yes ____ No

If there is one thing you could change about your marriage, what would it be?

_____

Is this a realistic change, and can you do anything to help it come about?

_____

_____

What have you done for your marriage lately?

_____

_____

What is the greatest problem area in your marriage to a bioparent?

_____

_____

Check on the warning signs of marriage failure.

Stepparent withdrawing from the stepfamily	____ Yes	____ No
Bioparent and stepchild spending most time together	____ Yes	____ No
Feelings your marriage was a mistake	____ Yes	____ No
Communication with stepfamily members decreasing	____ Yes	____ No
Frustration level with your spouse increasing	____ Yes	____ No
You feel "in love"	____ Yes	____ No
Feel you'll never fit in this stepfamily	____ Yes	____ No
Unable to see this stepfamily working in the future	____ Yes	____ No
Feel you are doing all of the work	____ Yes	____ No
Feeling you are the failure	____ Yes	____ No
Resent your stepchild	____ Yes	____ No

Now, review the list and identify which issues *you* can change today.

I can change how I feel about _____

_____

Keep listing what you can change, and then prioritize the list. What is the most important issue you need to change first?

_____

_____

Reward yourself with that biscotti for a job well done in focusing on your marriage and entering the world of identifying where you might still need work in your stepfamily.

My Stepfamily Journal

Chapter 10

Stage 6: Where Do We Still Need Work?

Okay, we've reached Stage 6. Yes! How are you doing? Do you feel more in control of your stepfamily and its direction? Good. Now there are some odds and ends that we need to discuss and must be included in your stepfamily plan. All stepfamilies face these same issues, which include:

- Bioparents feel inadequate at times in the stepfamily, and it's your job to understand this and be supportive. In this chapter, we'll explore why the bioparent might be feeling this way, and what you can do about it.

- Stepchildren are confused at times about what to call their step-parent. Should they call you stepmother or stepfather? Should they call you Mom or Dad? How comfortable do you feel with a title? This is something that is rarely discussed in stepfamilies, but it's important because these titles are terms of endearment, and carry meaning for you and your stepchild. So let's talk about it and plan ahead, making a decision about this for you and your stepfamily.

- An issue that is often mystifying in stepfamilies is finances. Why are finances such an issue in stepfamilies? How do you handle finances in a stepfamily? Finances are concerns in every family; however, in the stepfamily there is a separate set of concerns that need to be identified, discussed, and resolved to prevent further conflict about something that can easily be planned in advance.

- What are the advantages to stepfamilies? Are there *any* advantages to being in a stepfamily? I believe there are. Often, the negatives about stepfamilies are discussed because of the frequency and complicated nature of problem solving that needs to take place. But there are certain advantages, too. We will discuss them and how they can benefit you and your stepfamily members.

We've discussed many issues in the recent chapters. These issues include accepting your past family, creating your parenting team, alienation and its affects on your ability to move forward, creating your stepfamily vision, discipline (the most talked about stepparent issue!), extended family members plans, and what to do to ensure that your marriage survives your stepfamily; many important issues in your stepfamily that you may have encountered—or maybe not, just yet. These are all issues that we "steppies" share in this club, this unique group of people who have accepted the challenge of becoming "the stepparent."

These issues comprise the major obstacles and potential conflicts you may encounter in your stepfamily. The four issues that we'll discuss in this chapter represent areas of the stepfamily that are often asked about but not analyzed extensively by stepfamilies prior to the marriage. Let's take the time now to explore these areas and try to find answers that will work for your stepfamily.

Step 1: Understanding Why a Bioparent Feels Inadequate in the Stepfamily

There are actually a number of reasons why this might be happening. A bioparent has a very important and difficult job in the stepfamily. That job is to maintain a balance between you and their child. This can be an overwhelming task, and the bioparent has no training for this. The bioparent is often unprepared for the conflicts that occur between their child and you, and this creates an environment of uncertainty for the bioparent, and contributes to the guilt they might be feeling and disappointment with the spouse they have chosen. Sounds complicated? Oh yeah. Is it insurmountable? No. It is, in fact, correctable. The key is to correct the inadequacy feelings in enough time—or better yet, plan ahead for it—so that the marriage and stepfamily can work through this together.

The bioparent comes into the marriage, like you, expecting a long and happy life together. However, what generally happens is increased guilt about the choices they have made for their children. Why? Because if things go poorly in the marriage, the bioparent may see the stepfamily as damaging to her children, particularly if conflicts and problems escalate and no resolution is in sight.

The bioparent is human too and feels all of the emotions you do—just maybe at different times than you do. Sometimes you feel that you are the only one feeling inadequate or not up to the stepfamily challenge. But the bioparent experiences these emotions plus the added emotional load of worrying about the children's state of mind. A stepfamily is unique in that sense—it conjures up emotional sides of us we either didn't know existed or we'd rather not know existed! Frustration, anger, love, anxiety, inadequacy—each adult in a stepfamily marriage feels these emotions, not just you. So, this is a valuable opportunity to point out what you share with your spouse and build on that strength to help guide you both through the marriage and stepfamily journey. Building on this strength together can help your Stepfamily Plan become a reality created from both of your desires to maintain a solid marriage and a solid stepfamily well into your future. Let's look at how you and your spouse can pool your emotional strengths and plan together for your stepfamily.

You and your spouse are coming from different viewpoints in the stepfamily. This is an essential point for you to understand for the survival of your marriage and stepfamily. The bioparent is looking out for himself and his children. You are looking ahead for the adults, you and your spouse. Your goals are the same, but your means to get there will be different. This brings two separate strengths—strength in having the same goals and strength in diversity.

So what specific things may the bioparent feel inadequate about?

- The bioparent could feel guilty about the divorce and that the core family is no longer intact for their child.

- The bioparent may feel helpless when problems erupt in the step-family that they cannot fix, particularly the stepparent asking for more support. The bioparent may interpret this support as siding with the stepparent and betraying their child.

- The bioparent may resent the stepparent when things aren't working out.

- The bioparent may feel threatened by the stepparent parenting their child.

Bioparents will likely feel inadequate about how this stepfamily should work. A bioparent is hopeful that the stepparent and their child will get along, but generally have no fallback plan if this doesn't happen. Bioparents especially need a vision for the stepfamily. And little planning ahead leads to unresolved problems down the road. The stepparent generally takes the initiative to confront the problems in the stepfamily, and the bioparent tries to understand, but it's tough to balance the problems between their new spouse and their child. A bioparent often is ill-equipped to deal with the conflicts that arise. It's a new experience for them, too. There isn't a handbook on how to tolerate and accept an outsider into your child's family core—this is a big step that the bioparent takes and the rules are made up along the way. As a stepparent, you need to try to understand where your spouse is coming from. Do not take this responsibility lightly. The bioparent will be counting on you to fulfill this role that they've created for you within their family. You need to honor that role.

Case History: Kay and Luke

Luke and Kay were happily married, having joined their two families. Kay and Luke felt that they loved each other so much that they could handle any problems that came up. Gradually, both Luke and Kay started to doubt their original plan. They didn't anticipate the degree to which their children weren't getting along, and they also didn't anticipate how they would each begin to question each other's ability to resolve problems.

Luke and Kay felt that the creation of the stepfamily would add to their kids' sense of family, rather than take away from it. The thing they didn't anticipate was the reaction their kids had to this notion. The kids wanted to please their parents, so they tried to go along with this step-family idea. But when the reality of everyday life set in, the kids were living together, and they had yet another parent to listen to, the step-family illusion began to break down for Kay and Luke. Both of them began to question how they thought that bringing an outsider into the family core would work! Luke was disappointed in Kay for the way she handled certain situations with his kids and Kay felt the same way about Luke. Each felt their children were being hurt by this union, and neither knew how to fix it. So the problems got worse, the tension grew, and soon a once loving and nurtured marriage was beginning to crumble, which left the stepfamily status in a tenuous situation at best.

How was this resolved? Let's analyze the solution to this problem, one step at a time.

1. **Luke and Kay both outlined what their goals were for the stepfamily in the first place.** This is important because the adults need to refocus on the big picture and not stay bogged down in a single incident. The adults also need to regroup as a solid team.

2. **Once the original goals were identified and revisited, both Kay and Luke got out of the rut they were in and remembered why they wanted this stepfamily in the first place.** This is a refresher for both adults. Have this conversation over dinner at a quiet restaurant or at your favorite spot you went to before you were married. Rekindle that flame in both of you first.

3. **Both needed to recommit to their original goals.** Recommit yourselves to each other and to the goals of your stepfamily.

4. **Kay and Luke agreed to again parent as a team and consciously not blame each other for problems with the children.** Kay and Luke had been subconsciously blaming one another and doubting their choice for a spouse to share their kids with.

5. **Kay and Luke agreed to hold the stepchildren accountable for their actions.** This step is extremely important. Many step-families fail because the stepchild isn't held accountable for their behavior but rather the bioparent blames the stepparent for disciplining their child when the child needs to be corrected. This is a tough step for bioparents, but it's necessary to help make the stepfamily work.

6. **Kay and Luke then sat down with the kids, and outlined the original goals for the stepfamily.** Then they carefully laid out

each child's role in that without letting the children argue them out of it. The children need to understand who the parents are and that their job as stepchildren is to listen, follow the rules, and not treat the stepparent or their parent with disrespect. This step is equally important because *both* parents must talk with the stepchildren together because the stepchildren must get the idea that you are a team and that there will be no opportunity for them to split you apart on decisions.

7. **Each child was then asked to discuss their goal for the stepfamily.** This will help the stepchild understand that they have an opportunity for input and that they are expected to have a goal for the stepfamily. However, the stepchild is also to understand that input does not mean it will be their way.

8. **Each child was then asked to write down one thing they could do to support the stepfamily and help reduce the tension toward a balanced environment in the home.** Encourage your stepchild to create an idea of how they can help improve things. Nine chances out of ten, they know what they can do to make things better. Have them earn a position in the stepfamily and expect them to follow it.

9. **Kay and Luke also informed the stepchildren of the consequences if they were not following rules in the home.** Caution your stepchild that they have rules, and will be expected to follow them. If they choose not to follow your rules, they will need to face the consequences.

Kay and Luke followed this plan carefully and kept to it without question for one month. After that time, the atmosphere in the home had changed moderately and relationships had become more tolerable. Kay and Luke continued with this plan, adding and modifying where needed with the stepchildren, and making sure to support one another. After two months, the climate in their home had changed dramatically. The adults were acting in unison and neither Kay nor Luke doubted one another. By recommitting to their marriage and their goals for their stepfamily, they knew they could count on one another for support and did not have to question this. The stepchildren objected initially, still trying to control things by manipulating their parents, but with the new accountability that the stepchildren were held to and with Luke and Kay both sticking to their positions and not wavering, the stepchildren soon learned that the parents were in charge, and that the parents were serious about this stepfamily working with everyone having to give and sacrifice in some way. After all, isn't that what families do?

Every stepfamily is different; this time frame may be more or less in your stepfamily, depending on the severity of the conflicts and the personalities involved. However, if you follow this basic outline in problems by first taking a step back and revisiting your original goals, you can then slowly begin to create a plan for each problem you encounter by looking first at what is needed to resolve and examining what each member of the stepfamily must do in order to help resolve it.

Step 2: What Should Your Stepchild Call You?

This can be a sensitive issue in stepfamilies, particularly between the stepchild and you. What are the concerns around what a stepchild should call you?

- The stepchild wants to please your spouse, their bioparent, but simultaneously feel that they don't want to betray their other parent. You are in the middle of this tension.

- The stepchild may agree to call you what you want to be called because they don't know you very well and they don't want to create a conflict. However, your stepchild may resent you for this because they feel uncomfortable with the title and they would rather call you by your first name, allowing for a little distance in your relationship.

- The stepchild may be in a confused state because they don't want to offend anyone but they've got two stepparents (one married to their mom and the other married to their dad) who want them to each call them something different.

There may be an additional concern with this issue in your stepfamily. If so, certainly add that to the list.

Let's discuss each of these concerns in detail. There are obvious choices for what a stepchild may call you. If a child is younger than seven, the stepchild can call the stepparent "Dad number two" or "Mom number two," or "second dad" or "second mom." It's generally easier for younger children to incorporate the words "Mom" and "Dad" in some form. To reduce the confusion, children under seven should not call the stepparent by just "Mom" or "Dad," to distinguish the stepparent from their bioparent. For a child over seven, the first name of the stepparent is most commonly used. Certainly any of these choices are fine, however, let's also discuss what is inappropriate and unfair to the stepchild. Don't ask your stepchild to call you "Mom" or "Dad." They already have a mother and father (unless their mother or father is deceased or missing), and this may create an uncomfortable situation for them. The titles Mom and Dad mean a lot to children, and a stepchild should not be pushed into calling someone else the same titles as their bioparents. They may feel as though they are betraying their birth parents.

Be sure that your stepchildren are comfortable with what you are expecting them to call you. Sometimes your stepchild may want to please you and will go along with calling you by something they don't feel comfortable with. Your stepchild may not want to rock the boat, so she'll not say anything and just call you by whatever title you've asked her to.

Also, try not to confuse your stepchild by asking them to call you something completely different than the stepparent in their other home, if there is one. A stepchild can sometimes be expected to learn two completely separate routines and house rules and then be expected to call the two stepparents involved something different, too. Consistency is really the best policy for your stepchild, whether it relates to parenting or titles used in the households.

What is the bottom line on what your stepchild should call you? The best way to approach this in general is for you and your spouse to decide what the stepchild should call you, gather input through your parenting team about how your stepchild addresses the stepparent in the other household, and then you and your spouse discuss it with your stepchild. Everyone in your stepfamily should feel comfortable with the decision;1

14 therefore, input from your stepchild, if older than seven, should be considered. The stepchild must feel comfortable with what to call you. It'll make a huge difference in your relationship with your stepchild.

What does your stepchild call you?

Step 3: Treading the Murky Waters of Stepfamily Finances

Finances are a concern with every family; however, unique circumstances exist with stepfamily finances. Why? Because it's a true test of sharing. A bioparent and stepparent will be tested to their core about how far they would go in paying for someone else's child, or a stepparent will question themselves about it at the very least. And if the answer to the question is, "No, I don't want to share my money to pay for your child," an added sense of guilt is heaped on the stepparent. So, it comes down to more than just finances; it comes down to a test of how much the stepparent really loves the bioparent and his children. Should it come to this? No—but it does.

Adults in stepfamilies may feel that they've been taken advantage of in a previous relationship so money can become an incredibly sensitive issue. The thought of combining finances may be uncomfortable. There is also the question about whether the stepparent should contribute finances for the stepchild, particularly if the stepparent has his own children. But what about something everybody in the house will utilize, such as household expenses? Just how should the finances be handled in a stepfamily?

Finances should be included as part of your Stepfamily Plan, and I encourage you to create a financial plan with your spouse before the marriage if possible, but certainly as soon as possible. Finances may be the reason the first marriage broke up, so paying attention to finances in your stepfamily should be a priority.

How do you plan for stepfamily finances? As always, breaking down the problem into manageable pieces to solve one at a time is best.

- Money provokes emotion. Identify how each adult feels about money, how it should be earned, and how it should be spent. Who will plan the finances in the stepfamily? Who feels money is more important?

- Finances, quite simply, can be broken down into two major categories and should be planned for in advance.

  a. Household expenses (everyday expenses)

  b. Future retirement for you and your spouse

c. (Optional) What the stepparent will pay for the stepchild. A stepparent is not required to provide financially for the stepchild. This should be voluntary and only if the stepparent chooses to do this.

I suggest the following for a basic financial plan to follow:

- Set up three accounts: one separate account for each adult and a joint account where each adult contributes a certain previously agreed upon amount.

- See a financial planner for retirement and estate planning. Remember, keep this simple. Finances should not be a reason for stepfamily conflict. Finances can be planned ahead of time in an effort to prevent significant conflict in your stepfamily.

Review the following Financial Chart to help you identify first where your money is spent, and then to be proactive in determining where you want your money to be spent.

Financial Chart for Stepfamilies

Where is your money going now?

Adult #1		Adult #2	
Item	Amount per Week/Month/Year	**Item**	Amount per Week/Month/Year
Groceries	_____	Groceries	_____
Dinner out	_____	Dinner out	_____
Dry cleaning	_____	Dry cleaning	_____
Clothing	_____	Clothing	_____
Electric bill	_____	Electric bill	_____
Vacations	_____	Vacations	_____
_____	_____	_____	_____
_____	_____	_____	_____
_____	_____	_____	_____

Track your expenses for six months and review this every month. First, know where each partner's money is going and then redo the chart and plan for the next year, and so on. Better yet, take this completed chart to a financial advisor and work out a reasonable financial plan for your stepfamily to be sure:

- each adult feels they are contributing fairly

- that no one spouse is feeling overburdened with paying more or less

- to review this every six months to see if each adult still feels they are paying their fair share

What about unique situations such as the bioparent wanting their child to attend a private school when the stepparent's child attends public school? A good rule to abide by in stepfamilies for extraordinary situations is that the bioparent should be prepared to understand that the stepparent is not required to contribute, unless of course the stepparent wants to.

Step 4: Yes, There are Advantages to Being in a Stepfamily

When we talk about stepfamilies, we don't often discuss the advantages to being in a stepfamily situation. Discussions about stepfamilies tend to be dominated by the conflicts that arise rather than about the positives and advantages that stepfamilies afford the stepfamily members. Advantages do exist for those involved in a stepfamily, particularly for the stepchild. These advantages include the following:

The stepchild learns to navigate relationships at an earlier age. A stepchild has the opportunity to learn how relationships work in a stepfamily at a much earlier age than otherwise. Why? Because a stepchild learns that relationships with adults are not all based on unconditional nurturing and bonding. A stepchild learns that an adult may not immediately respond to them consistently with praise or even acceptance. They learn that their responses may be censored by an adult, namely the stepparent, who is not related to the stepchild and that how they verbally approach and respond to people will affect whether the relationship will thrive or not. This is an advantage to the stepchild because the stepchild will engage in the outside world prepared to handle the disagreements and conflicts that occur in relationships at school, in the workplace, or even with their in-laws when they choose to marry.

The stepchild learns appropriate boundaries at an earlier age. The stepchild learns to respect others' boundaries in a stepfamily. Why? Because a stepchild will have limits on anything from when and how they will be able to interrupt conversations with their bioparent and the stepparent to when and how they will be able to enter their parents' bedroom. The stepchild will be expected to be conscious of their actions when talking or entering a room. They will be expected to honor certain time restrictions, such as no telephone calls after 9 P.M., and further, these restrictions may be the stepparent's idea and not their bioparent's. The stepchild also will learn the consequences of violating boundaries because they will be held accountable. This is advantageous for the stepchild because they will handle relationships in the outside world with a greater degree of respect and maturity, having learned this in the home, rather than with their first roommate, for example.

The stepchild sees and understands differences between how adults act and react. Why is this important for your stepchild? Because they will understand at an earlier age how to conduct themselves with maturity in order to experience more balanced and happy relationships with others. Your stepchild will have you as a mentor in learning how to conduct themselves appropriately as an adult and maybe will learn a few things they won't want to express. They will absorb what you say and how you say it, whether you're positive or negative. You are not only a stepparent to your stepchild but also a key adult in their lives to help guide them toward behaving and functioning as a functional adult who will have their own family one day. You must remember that your stepchild is watching you, even though they may not let you know this. You are a mentor, and this is a job you need to take seriously.

The greatest advantage for a stepparent and the bioparent is the opportunity for a second chance. Yes, there is an advantage for the bioparent and you. This is an opportunity for a second chance at marriage and family and a second chance at happiness. The beauty of this advantage is that you can control and maintain it. Whatever circumstances affected you in your previous relationships, you have a redeeming experience awaiting you in the stepfamily. And you have the opportunity to change things about yourself that you know didn't work in a previous relationship. You can improve yourself, and in the process, build a successful subsequent marriage and family.

A stepfamily situation allows a stepparent a chance to understand who they are as individuals. We don't often experience opportunities that force us to look at ourselves with the genuineness and honesty that stepfamilies require. In a stepfamily, you reveal yourself not only to your spouse but also to their children. Children are perceptive; they will see who you are and be curious about your motives. Being a stepparent requires that we be conscious about how we speak, how we act, and how we handle situations—all in front of an audience. You may begin to understand your own weaknesses in relationship building and learn to analyze what is helpful or harmful in how you approach relationships. This is an advantage because it allows you an opportunity to improve *you*—and to do this in an environment with people who care about you and want to make a family with you. As you become the person you want and know you need to be, your relationships in other parts of your life will improve. It can be an uncomfortable but rewarding experience. If you experience this in your stepfamily, I strongly encourage you to embrace this opportunity and not withdraw from it. If you allow yourself to be open to your own weaknesses and to changing them, you are helping not only yourself but your stepfamily members as well.

Identify one advantage you have experienced in your stepfamily.

_____

_____

_____

Share this advantage with your stepfamily members and discuss it as a stepfamily. You may open their eyes to positives in your stepfamily that they had not considered before your discussion.

Quick Stage 6 Summary

Step 1: Bioparent Feeling Inadequate

Is the bioparent feeling inadequate because of:

Guilt _____ Yes _____ No

Resents you _____ Yes _____ No

Threatened by you parenting _____ Yes _____ No

Add your own: _____

_____

_____

If there is one thing the bioparent would change about the stepfamily, what would it be? _____

_____

_____

_____

Step 2: What Should Your Stepchild Call You?

What does your stepchild call you now? _____

_____

Are you comfortable with this?

____ Yes, it's okay   ____ No, I'd rather she/he call me _____

If no, when will you discuss this with your stepchild?

Today ____

Tomorrow ____

As soon as I get a minute ____

Step 3: Stepfamily Finances

We have no problems with finances in our stepfamily ____

We had some problems but have worked them out ____. If so, how?

_____

_____

We have severe financial problems in our stepfamily ____

I will complete and use the financial chart regularly ____ Yes ____ No

I will see a financial advisor for help ____ Yes ____ No

I will make a plan for our finances this year ____ Yes ____ No

Step 4: Advantages to Being in a Stepfamily

What are the specific advantages to being in your stepfamily? Each member should think of advantages from their own standpoint.

Stepparent _____

_____

_____

Stepchild _____

_____

_____

Bioparent _____

_____

_____

In this chapter, we covered common areas where your stepfamily might still need work. If your stepfamily specifically needs work in any area, please be sure to detail that in your journal. You also have the option of contacting me directly at www.docsuzen.com for further help in identifying, clarifying, and resolving that issue. You're doing some great work here for you and your stepfamily by openly confronting and problem solving these issues that can so often lead to the deterioration of stepfamilies.

Congratulations on your preventive efforts in your stepfamily. Now, take a breath or a short break if you need to, and let's dive into the exciting and creative challenges for you in the next chapter by creating your stepfamily traditions!

My Stepfamily Journal

Chapter 11

Stage 7: Create Your Stepfamily Traditions

Now comes the fun part! You get to cut and paste traditions from the past family, merge them with your own past family, and create your very own stepfamily traditions. Why is it important to establish stepfamily traditions? In my work with stepfamilies, it has become increasingly apparent that stepparents want to feel cemented into their new stepfamily, and one of the best ways to accomplish this is by acknowledging stepparents' wishes for traditions.

Many stepparents feel that they are expected to adapt to all of their new spouse's and stepchild's traditions. Stepparents often feel that their needs and desires for their own traditions with their new spouse go unacknowledged. This often results in stepparents feeling inadequate and less important in their role in the stepfamily, which often leads to the destruction of the stepfamily. Such a simple idea—equality for every member of the stepfamily, right? Your stepfamily doesn't have to fall victim to this exclusion because you can change the pattern. How? You can play an integral part in establishing new family traditions just for your stepfamily. But first, let's be clear about what a stepfamily tradition is, what it means, and discuss the importance of what stepfamily traditions represent for you and members of your stepfamily.

Stepfamily Traditions and Why They're Important

A tradition is a family event marked by the family doing it *together* and believing in the continuity of the event. Traditions derive from past experience and help shape the present. The philosophy behind traditions comes from families building their histories together. It's these same traditions that are often so difficult to leave behind in a divorce or other type of family separation. It's difficult for adults to experience the loss of traditions and their link to the previous family. If this is difficult for an adult member in a divorce situation, imagine how difficult it could be for your stepchild. You might want to jump right into the stepfamily, starting off with changing the existing traditions and establishing new stepfamily traditions at holidays and birthdays. But before you do that—wait, because you may be jumping into rejection from your spouse and stepchild because you're not considering *their* needs as well as your own. Sometimes stepparents move too quickly, eliminating past family traditions that didn't feel comfortable for them. The problem occurs when stepparents attempt this without considering the feelings of their spouse and stepchild or underestimate the depth of what these existing traditions meant to their spouse and stepchild. This can cause significant conflict in the stepfamily. Your spouse may feel that they married someone who doesn't care about what is important to them, and your stepchild may feel that you are mean and uncaring as well. There is a better way to handle this with your stepfamily members.

Family traditions are sacred events. You must approach modifying them delicately and with sensitivity. You must be diplomatic, patient, and as open minded and tolerant as possible. Why? Because you may just find yourself participating in the old traditions, as well as creating your own.

Exploring Your Own Family Traditions

Think of your own family and what traditions you held sacred and honored annually. There are any number and variety of traditions that families create and continue. Traditions can evolve around religious holidays, political holidays, wedding anniversaries, birthdays, or annual golf, shopping, or baseball tournaments. Whatever interests your immediate family had, you may have established traditions around these interests or events that were important milestones for your family.

Exercise: Reviewing Your Family Traditions

Let's take a look at the traditions you enjoyed in your immediate family. Take a moment now and list the traditions that were important to you from your family of origin.

- _____
  _____

- _____
  _____

- _____
  _____

- _____
  _____

- _____
  _____

Repeat this exercise for your spouse also. Take a moment now and have your spouse list traditions that were important in her family while growing up.

- _____
  _____

- _____
  _____

- _____
  _____

- _____

• _____

Traditions Can Be a Way of Maintaining Your Stepfamily

Though at times traditions seem insignificant to some family members, the fact is that traditions are a very important element in the development and maintenance of families. Maintaining your stepfamily will be a full-time job for you and your stepfamily members. Creating traditions that your stepfamily can look forward to and participate in together encourages your stepfamily to stay together and stay strong. This is a great tool to utilize as maintenance, and particularly as preventive maintenance.

Traditions Can Encourage Bonding in Your Stepfamily

Traditions also serve an important role in bonding families together. This is important for traditional families but even more important for stepfamilies. Why? Because of the increased potential for conflict in stepfamilies, which can lead to the stepfamily falling apart. Traditions provide a symbol for your stepfamily; they are a celebration of the stepfamily not just being together, but remaining together each year to keep the symbol of their stepfamily strong. Traditions provide wonderful memories for your stepchild, as well as for you and your spouse. And they are events all members of your stepfamily can participate in.

Step 1: Planning For Stepfamily Traditions

How should you start planning for your own stepfamily traditions? Well, first you want to honor the traditions that both you and your spouse bring to your marriage. Each of your family traditions are important and should continue as before, but both you and your spouse need to make adjustments to each other's family traditions. You each need to accept your past traditions and support those traditions that you want to perpetuate. For example, at Christmas, if your spouse and stepchild always celebrated midnight Mass with your spouse's parents, and they both want to continue this. But what about you? You may have celebrated Christmas by going to your parent's house and opening gifts on Christmas Eve, and you'd like to continue doing that. Which tradition should continue?

The easy answer is to try and keep traditions as close to what they were for the stepchild. Why? Because you're an adult, you can compromise with your spouse for the sake of the stepchild, and you have the power to create new traditions for your stepfamily. It's important for your stepchild to be able to continue some of the same traditions that they enjoyed prior to the development of the stepfamily. But it is equally important that your stepchild also understand that your stepfamily will have new traditions as well. In creating new traditions for your stepfamily, it's important that you take the stepchild's interests into consideration. Traditions are for kids—they help cement their family memories well into adulthood. You want the same for your stepfamily, but understand that your stepchild has a history *prior* to the stepfamily, just like you did. Don't pressure your stepchild to make adjustments that are completely different from what they are used to and what they are familiar with. Place the stepchild's needs before your own in this category. Once you have done this, you may then begin to create new stepfamily traditions. But how do you know what traditions existed before and which traditions can or cannot be tampered with?

Exercise: Review Traditions Your Spouse and Stepchild Have Shared

Let's do another list. Have your spouse make a list of traditions that he or she feels are important and has shared with their child throughout their lives. An example might be a weekend at a family cottage every summer.

- _____

    _____

- _____

    _____

- _____

    _____

• _____

_____

• _____

_____

Now, have your stepchild make a list of traditions they hold special in their lives. What does your stepchild value as family memories?

• _____

_____

• _____

_____

• _____

_____

• _____

_____

• _____

_____

You may need to help your stepchild with this exercise and emphasize why it's important. Also, you will need to explain how they can help create new traditions for the stepfamily. This list is important for your spouse because they may feel that certain traditions are important to their child, but the child feels differently. Knowing this in advance might save precious compromising time in the future. Why? Because your spouse may be defending a tradition that her stepchild doesn't care about and vice versa. Be clear with your stepchild that your goal is to enhance or build on family traditions and *not* to eliminate them.

These lists will give you and your stepfamily members a clear picture of what types of traditions your families felt were important and may want to continue. They may be similar or vastly different. In either case, this is a strength for your stepfamily because you can build on similar interests or be introduced to new ideas.

Step 2: Acknowledging These Traditions

This integration sounds complicated, but there are simple steps that you can take in your stepfamily plan to:

1. Be sure everyone's viewpoint is considered, and

2. Avoid offense by acknowledging all the traditions.

Exercise: Merging Old Traditions into the New

Put all of the lists together that you and your stepfamily members created. In this exercise, you will prioritize your traditions by following these strategies:

- First, designate which traditions may be similar—some may be exactly the same. For example, each of you may prefer to celebrate birthdays quietly at home with the family.

- Designate those traditions that are very different and whose integration will need to be discussed because they simply may not work. For example, if family birthdays are celebrated only at your spouse's ex-in-law's home, that may cause a problem for you.

- Mark those traditions that are a challenge to either your spouse, your stepchild, or you but are still doable. These will need to be discussed to determine whether they will continue in your stepfamily.

- Finally, mark those traditions that are neutral and will cause no conflict.

Use the following list to prioritize existing traditions:

- _____

  _____

- _____

  _____

- _____

  _____

- _____

- _____

- _____

- _____

- _____

- _____

All stepfamily members must agree on prioritizing traditions. You and your stepfamily members will discuss these traditions and plan ahead for how to deal with them. Of course, the traditions that may cause conflict will be the traditions that will require the greatest amount of problem solving and discussion. You will need to decide as a stepfamily how you will continue to honor existing traditions that may be conflictual. For example, let's take the birthday celebration example above. If your stepchild's birthday was previously celebrated at your spouse's ex-in-law's home, this may be uncomfortable for your new stepfamily and you. You will still want your stepchild's birthday to be celebrated, but you may suggest that this party now be held at your home to signify your stepfamily's significance in the extended family or at a more neutral place where the ex-spouse doesn't have so much power.

Now, clearly the personalities and factors involved will vary in each stepfamily. As the stepparent, you need to decide your comfort level with your spouse and stepchild's traditions and proceed with compromising suggestions. Remember to proceed with caution. Your goal here is to create new and long-lasting bonds with your stepfamily members and not to alienate anyone.

What is the best way to approach this? Proactively, by confronting uncomfortable situations *before* they occur, developing a plan where each stepfamily member can have their needs met as much as possible. But remember, you don't get everything that you want! Appreciate what compromise you can achieve and be understanding of where you need to be.

Case History: Brenna and Jed

Jed and Brenna were married after dating for two years. Brenna knew each of Jed's family traditions with his own family and those shared with her stepchild in Jed's previous marriage and family. She was fine with most of the traditions, but there was one that was uncomfortable and she felt that she needed to have changed. This tradition involved a kayaking trip that Jed took his daughter, Dana, on every year. The problem came in because Brenna had a fear of the water. Brenna felt excluded from this trip because of her fear of water, and as a result, she started to resent Jed and Dana discussing this trip annually and reminiscing about the memories of trips from recent years. Brenna felt that Jed was being insensitive to her fears and that Jed needed to change this tradition to an annual trip where Brenna could be included.

Jed was unwilling to change the tradition with Dana. This is not uncommon with bioparents and stepparents need to understand this. Your spouse wants his child to have fond family memories. So what did Brenna and Jed do? Rather than asking Jed to stop or change something that he enjoyed and cherished with Dana, the solution was to compromise. How? Jed could continue his kayaking trip with Dana, but he also needed to start a new tradition like this that included Brenna. By compromising, Jed could keep his tradition with his daughter and Brenna could not only enjoy an annual trip with her stepfamily but also have a new stepfamily tradition created. This allowed Brenna to feel that her presence is important in the stepfamily *and* that her needs are acknowledged. There is a third benefit, and that is to the stepchild. Not only does Jed's daughter get to maintain the trip with her father, but she also enjoys a second annual adventure!

This scenario frequently plays out in stepfamilies. The problem comes in when adults each feel they either don't need to compromise or one adult feels they are always doing the compromising. By building your Stepfamily Plan, you will be noting who compromises and when. It is important that you keep track of this because you will then visually see how often each of you compromises. This sounds petty, but it's these kinds of stressors that build in stepfamilies and lead to their breakdown. It is vitally important that each adult be open to discussion, compromise, and change in stepfamilies. This should be included in the wedding vows for marriages! As the stepparent, you are not expected to do all of the changing, compromising, and adapting. Your spouse needs to accept this responsibility, just as you do. But it's a verbal commitment that each of you need to make to each other and to the stepfamily.

What do you do if one of you is not cooperating in compromise? The first thing you need to do is review your Stepfamily Plan to be sure whose turn it is to compromise. Review the last conflict you encountered, and determine who compromised or changed the last time for the survival of the stepfamily. If it was your spouse, then you need to strongly consider compromising on this one. The bottom line is that if one spouse is doing the compromising and adapting and is frustrated by the situation, this is not only unfair, but it's not in the best interest of the stepfamily. If you or your spouse refuse to compromise on *anything*, then this is a red flag for possible serious commitment challenges to your stepfamily. I would recommend seeking professional counseling if this is occurring to determine the reasons why and how to overcome this intransigence for the sake of your stepfamily's future.

Additional Ways to Merge Old Traditions with the New

So, merging traditions can occur like it did with Jed and Brenna above. What are other ways to merge traditions? Let's look at an example in your stepfamily.

Exercise: Modifying, Changing, and Adapting Your Stepfamily Traditions

First, write down a tradition that you feel needs to be modified in your stepfamily.

A tradition in my stepfamily that needs change is: _____

_____

_____

_____

_____

Now, both you and your spouse need to offer suggestions for how this tradition can be changed by merging it to meet all stepfamily members' needs.

Stepparent

I feel this tradition can be changed by: _____

_____

_____

_____

Bioparent

I feel this tradition can be changed by: _____

_____

_____

_____

Now let's merge this tradition. Taking your ideas and your spouse's input, both of you describe a realistic solution to merging this tradition in your stepfamily that is workable *and* that each of you can live with.

We will merge this tradition and the new tradition will now be: _____

_____

_____

_____

Repeat this process through each and every tradition that you or your spouse feel needs revamping in order to encourage and maintain the success of your stepfamily. Be sure to discuss this process and it's results in your stepfamily journal and review this annually to determine if you and your spouse feel any change is needed.

Create New Stepfamily Traditions for Now and into the Future

As a stepparent, you want your stepfamily to experience special moments and celebrate milestones or events that you feel are unique to you. In my work with stepparents, I frequently hear the frustration that stepparents feel when they are "expected" to adapt to the traditions and routines that their spouse already had established with his or her child. You may feel this same way in your stepfamily. In general, stepparents want to honor these traditions, and the problem does not begin there. The problem occurs when a stepparent feels that their spouse does not want to or is unwilling to recognize their needs as far as traditions for the stepfamily. This begs the questions, "Why are new traditions so important to stepparents?"

The answer represents the heart of conflict in the stepfamily that is the basis for this book—because the stepparent needs, deserves, requests, and requires a "place" in the stepfamily. Bioparents, please pay attention! As a stepparent, you need to be assured that your needs will be met—maybe not all of them and to the extent that you'd like, but in a reasonable and workable fashion.

It's perfectly reasonable for you to want traditions in your step-family. After all, you are in this for the long run and you know the value and importance of traditions for longevity in stepfamilies. One of the most reasonable ways to assert yourself and solidify your position in the stepfamily is to create new stepfamily traditions not only for the present but to survive well into your stepfamily's future.

For traditions already established such as Christmas and Thanks-giving, the best strategy is to try and adapt as best you can to your spouse and stepchild. However, where the opportunity presents itself for you as the stepparent to be proactive is in suggesting a completely new tradition that your stepchild and spouse have not participated in before. This can be a tradition created solely by you. You own it and take charge of it. Here are a couple of suggestions to get you started.

- Think about starting a tradition on Father's Day if your spouse is the biofather or Mother's Day if your spouse is the biomother.

- Create an annual tradition on Stepfamily Day (September 16).

- Rent a cabin for the third week in August on an annual basis for your stepfamily to close the summer and welcome in autumn.

- Designate the second week of January for a ski outing.

- Be there for the opening first weekend of fishing every year.

- Meet in a designated city every year as a stepfamily with extended family.

- Attend a local festival every year as a stepfamily.

- Have a barbecue on Labor Day every year at your house.

- Go to the lake every Memorial Day and have a picnic.

How do you start planning for new stepfamily traditions? Like so many other problem-solving strategies in the stepfamily, you should include a well-thought-out plan, discussion with other stepfamily members, and compromise. The first question you need to ask is: What do you want to celebrate in your stepfamily?

Exercise: What Should You Celebrate?

Using the spaces below, indicate which holidays throughout the year you and your stepfamily members would like to celebrate as a stepfamily. They can be major holidays and/or special mini holidays and events that you enjoy as a stepfamily.

- _____

- _____

- _____

- _____

- _____

- _____

- _____

- _____

- _____

Now, in your journal write a brief scenario of each tradition and how you would like your stepfamily to celebrate it. For example:

Tradition 1: St. Patrick's Day

Now, list the when, where, and who.

When: March 17, 2003

Where: O'Leary's Pub, Irish Street, Irishtown, USA

Who: Each stepfamily member should be listed and others you would like present.

Do this for every tradition listed above. For each tradition, you will need to discuss this developing scenario with your stepfamily members.

Congratulations on identifying family-of-origin traditions and step-family traditions. So often stepparents will want to implement their new stepfamily traditions in their stepfamilies without planning ahead and as a result, the new stepfamily traditions are not well received by the step-family members. This can become a frustrating point for stepparents who then feel that their needs are not being met in the stepfamily, but you have taken the first step toward preventing that feeling of unmet needs. Good for you. By planning ahead and negotiating for what you need as a stepparent, your needs will be better received by the people you deeply care about in your stepfamily. This helps you be proactive and solidify your position in the stepfamily.

Let's move on and complete the summary now based on what you have learned in the chapter.

Quick Stage 7 Summary

Create Your Stepfamily Traditions

Do you feel creating new stepfamily traditions is important?
_____ Yes _____ No

If yes, briefly describe your reason(s) why.

_____

_____

_____

What does creating a stepfamily tradition mean to you?

_____

_____

_____

Rate the process of identifying, merging, and/or creating new traditions in your stepfamily.

Extremely difficult   _____

A little bumpy, but we accomplished this as a family   _____

Smooth—it went better than I thought   _____

My Stepfamily Journal

Chapter 12

Stage 8: How Do I Maintain My Stepfamily Plan?

Here we are at Stage 8. You have come such a long way. Congratulations. You have made progress in the success of your stepfamily just by reading this book and by working through this plan with your stepfamily members. You've seen where opportunities exist for you to be proactive and take charge in your stepfamily. It's important that you feel you are a significant and valued member of your stepfamily. But you must also take the good with the bad. To have a position of value in any group, you need to accept any consequences that come with assertive behavior. For example, if you assert yourself in your stepfamily, you may experience resistance from your stepfamily members. It is important that you understand this and accept and handle any consequences as a result.

The best way to maintain any working plan is to review and evaluate the plan periodically to be sure it is:

- effective,

- meeting the needs of the people involved,

- and still serving its original purpose.

Reviewing your Stepfamily Plan periodically can ensure that your stepfamily is moving along in the direction you had planned and intended. Review and evaluation also provides opportunities to change, modify, and adapt the plan to changes that occur in your stepfamily. The effectiveness of the Stepfamily Plan will be determined by you and your stepfamily members' participation. Taking a proactive approach, you can control the degree of effectiveness of your Stepfamily Plan, and the periodic evaluations provide an excellent opportunity to work on things as they come up. Meeting the needs of the people involved in your Stepfamily Plan is significant because it a measure of how productive your Stepfamily Plan has been, currently is, and will be in the future. It is essential that the Stepfamily Plan is meeting the needs of the people involved. If not, you must point this out and work together to modify toward improvement. The Stepfamily Plan is your guide toward a successful stepfamily. Take care of it, just as you would anything of value to your stepfamily. And finally, be sure the Stepfamily Plan continues to serve its original purpose. Sometimes throughout the difficulties and frustrating times in stepfamilies, it becomes easy to overlook the original goal and purpose of your stepfamily. Don't let that happen to you. You can prevent this through proactivity, planning ahead, *and* by keeping a visible reminder of the goal of your Stepfamily Plan in full sight—maybe the refrigerator door, the notepad on the wall by the telephone, or anywhere in your home that you can continually see what you and your stepfamily members are working toward.

Step 1: Use Your Stepfamily Plan As a Working Plan

Your Stepfamily Plan should be a working plan. That is, after all of the work you have put into this plan, you need to use it often—every day— to reap the many benefits from it. For example, just as keeping the goal of your plan is important, keep your completed Stepfamily Plan in visible sight—on your coffee table, next to your computer, or in the bathroom—any place in your home where it will be a visible reminder to you of your commitment to your stepfamily and it's successes and where stepfamily members have a chance to read it. Discuss it often with your stepfamily members. Set a weekly, bi-weekly, or monthly time to review your plan and be sure all members of your stepfamily are working on their part. These meetings will keep your Stepfamily Plan alive in your stepfamily, particularly when you are confronted with an issue that may have taken you off guard. A key to the success of your Stepfamily Plan will be to keep referring to it, communicating about it, and using it. Your Stepfamily Plan is the blueprint, the layout of your stepfamily. But even with the best-laid plans, some events may surprise you, and you may be unsure of how to effectively handle the situation. But having laid out your Stepfamily Plan in detail, you will already have the tools to handle any unexpected conflict that may occur.

Let's review the tools of your Stepfamily Plan:

- Planning ahead;

- Breaking down each problem and rebuilding it back up, one step at a time;

- Being supportive and understanding of your stepfamily members.

Step 2: Review Your Stepfamily Plan

Now let's review your Stepfamily Plan. To maintain your stepfamily and ensure a solid, balanced future, it's important that you review the Stepfamily Plan regularly. But just how regularly should you review your plan?

Each section of your Stepfamily Plan will require evaluation at different intervals due to the various issues at each stage. To be completely effective, let's review each category of your Stepfamily's Plan to determine the best time periods to review, modify, and change if needed. Be sure to be honest and genuine in your review and evaluation of your Stepfamily Plan.

Your Stepfamily Plan Review

Stage 1: Make Peace with Your Family's Past

Have you been able to make peace with your family's past?
____ Yes ____ No

If no, what do you need to do to continue to achieve past family acceptance?

_____

_____

Review this every three months and be sure to record the progress in your Stepfamily Journal.

Create (or have created) your Parenting Team by _____ (date)

The members are:

_____ Stepparent

_____ Bioparent

_____ Bioparent

_____ Other Stepparent

_____ Other (maybe grandparents if applicable)

Goals for my Parenting Team include:

- _____

- _____

- _____

- _____

Remember to keep the best interests of the child at the forefront of this team.

Review the above goals by: _____ (date)

This can be reviewed every three months in the first year of your Stepfamily Plan and every six months in the second and third years. Thereafter, the goals should be reviewed annually.

Stage 2: Observe, Listen, and Learn

Stepfamily Vision

In Stage 2, you learned about your stepfamily members and created your stepfamily vision. The best way to maintain this stage is to review at regular intervals just how your family is doing at meeting your stepfamily vision. After learning about your stepfamily members and knowing more about how they might act/react to situations, you will be better prepared to understand your stepfamily's needs for the future to adapt, modify, and make change where needed. Another big issue in Stage 2 is the issue of alienation. It's important that you review the intensity of alienation that you are feeling. Once knowing this, you can ask your stepfamily members for what you need to help correct it.

Alienation

How often should you evaluate your feelings of alienation? You should evaluate this every three weeks or less, depending on how intense this feeling may be for you. Alienation can be a reason for stepparents wanting out of their marriage and stepfamily, so it's an issue that you must keep your eye on. Ask yourself the following questions when you evaluate your feelings of alienation:

- Are you feeling alienated? ____ Yes ____ No

- If yes, how significant is it?

    a. It's controlling my life ____

    b. It's there, and I need it to change ____

    c. It's there, but I can still function ____

    d. Describe the level of *your* alienation: _____

    _____

Circle the words or phrases that apply to how you are feeling in regard to alienation.

Alone

Withdrawn

Jealous of the others' relationships together

Left out

Inferior

Frustrated

Angry

Like I made a mistake marrying this person

If you circled three or more of these, you are experiencing extreme difficulty with alienation. I encourage you to seek outside professional help to enable you to deal with this problem.

Stage 3: Assert Your Role in the Stepfamily

Discipline Review

Discipline is the most asked-about issue in stepparenting and step-families. Should you do it? Should you not do it? How will your spouse feel about this? What kind of disciplinarian should you be? These and many additional questions probably have come up about this issue.

In order to maintain the issue of discipline in your stepfamily, you are going to need to evaluate this. How often? Well, the need for discipline is going to take place in your stepfamily often, so initially you may need to evaluate the disciplining daily. Check with your spouse at the end of the day. Discuss how you are feeling and how she is feeling about how you are doing with disciplining her child. Talk about ways that you can improve if needed. If your spouse feels you can improve, ask for specifics. Take an example of a case where you have disciplined and ask your spouse for help in doing it better the next time. Do role playing so that your spouse can show you how he or she would handle the situation. When you role play, you play the role of the stepchild and your spouse can be you. It's like a practice session for how to discipline. This is often helpful in letting you see where you may have made a mistake and how to correct it next time.

Daily discussions about discipline with your spouse gives both of you:

- An opportunity to share an incredibly important job in the step-family as you work as a team;

- Strength in your marriage and commitment to each other;

- An equal position in the stepfamily as adult, spouse, and parent;

- A reduction in your feelings of alienation.

Once you feel the daily discussions and "practice sessions" have been helpful and have built your confidence, you can go to weekly discussions, then bi-weekly and monthly, depending on how much more work and how much more confidence you feel you will need.

Stage 4: Navigate the Extended Family Member Circuit

In Stage 4, we talked about extended family members and ways to navigate this circuit to help cement your position in the stepfamily. It's helpful to maintain your relationships with the extended family members to help support your stepfamily's future. You should evaluate your extended family member relationships periodically. Like any relationship, you need to tend and nurture them so that the relationships grow strong and healthy. How should you maintain your relationships with your extended family members, and how often should "maintenance" take place?

Your extended family member relationships, although important, require less frequent review and analysis than an issue like discipline, which is present in your stepfamily on a daily basis. Unless the extended stepfamily members are living with you, it is necessary to review your relationships with extended family members every three months for the first year of your Stepfamily Plan, at six month intervals into the second and third year of the plan, and annually thereafter. What should you review about extended family members?

First, look at the goals for the extended family members and see if these goals have been met or still need work.

Are your extended family members on both sides supportive of your stepfamily? _____ Yes _____ No   If no, what needs to happen for them to be supportive of your stepfamlly?

_____

_____

_____

What can you do to help create this change?

_____

_____

Are your extended family members a resource of strength for your stepfamily? _____ Yes _____ No   If no, what needs to happen for them to be a resource of strength?

_____

_____

What can you do to help create this change? What is the most important quality that your extended family has brought to your stepfamily?

_____

_____

What is the most important quality that your stepchild's extended family has brought to your stepfamily?

_____

_____

Review this information at the intervals suggested. Update and modify this information until you have reached a comfort level that you can live with.

Stage 5: Will My Marriage Survive This?

What can you do to maintain your marriage? You and your spouse can maintain your marriage daily. You can also attend marriage retreats that are offered through the Internet, through your church, or through various professional counseling centers throughout the country and the world. Marriage retreats are a great booster shot for your marriage. Try to find a retreat that focuses on stepfamily marriages, which will be most effective and beneficial to your union.

Make a list of things that you can do today to make your marriage better.

1. _____

_____

2. _____

_____

3. _____

_____

4. _____

_____

5. _____

_____

Have your spouse make a list.

1. _____

_____

2. _____

_____

3. _____

_____

4. _____

_____

5. _____

_____

Compare your lists, and you might be surprised at the differences or similarities in your thoughts about your marriage. Select three issues to prioritize, determine who can change it, and create a deadline to achieve the change.

Prioritize the Issues that need work:

1. _____

Who will/can change this issue?

_____

_____

Deadline to achieve the change:

_____

2. _____

Who will/can change this issue?

_____

_____

Deadline to achieve the change:

_____

3. _____

Who will/can change this issue?

_____

_____

Deadline to achieve the change:

_____

Stage 6: Where Do We Still Need Work?

Stage 6 is an exercise in maintenance by itself. Although issues touched on in Stage 6 are universal and affect all stepfamilies, you may have specific issues that your stepfamily still needs to work on. It's those customized issues that affect your stepfamily that you need to focus on in maintaining this stage.

Make a list of concerns that you have right now with your stepfamily.

1. _____

Who will/can change this issue?

_____

_____

Deadline to achieve the change:

_____

2. _____

Who will/can change this issue?

_____

_____

Deadline to achieve the change:

_____

3. _____

Who will/can change this issue?

_____

_____

Deadline to achieve the change:

_____

4. _____

Who will/can change this issue?

_____

_____

Deadline to achieve the change:

_____

Evaluate each concern as to what needs to be done to change it, who needs to change it, and a timeline for when this needs to be accomplished. Keep a chart of the progress, and check back weekly or bi-weekly at the start to be sure you're progressing in the right direction. Once you feel confident that your stepfamily is moving ahead in the right direction, you can evaluate your concerns every three months, then six months, and finally annually after that.

Stage 7: Create Your Stepfamily Traditions

All family traditions are special. Creating new stepfamily traditions is a great way for you to not only continue the past traditions but develop new ones customized just for your stepfamily. But how do you maintain these traditions and keep them special to you and your stepfamily?

Maintaining your stepfamily traditions allows you the opportunity to evaluate the new traditions you've created, determine if the tradition is working for your stepfamily, and whether it's fulfilling the original goal. If the traditions you've created are not fulfilling to your stepfamily, through maintenance you can change and improve your stepfamily traditions. What should you do first?

Review your Stepfamily Plan and the section on creating new stepfamily traditions. Take a look at the new traditions that you and your stepfamily have created. Take a moment now to review those traditions:

1. _____

2. _____

3. _____

4. _____

5. _____

6 _____

7. _____

8. _____

9. _____

10. _____

Evaluate which traditions are working well. Now, mark those traditions that need some tender loving care to be more successful. Remember that as your stepchild grows older, you may need to eliminate some traditions, such as attending the annual Little League softball tournament as a family. So in maintaining your Stepfamily Plan, you may find that you eliminate and perhaps replace some traditions as your stepfamily grows old together.

Each stepfamily member should provide valid and honest input about how they feel about the traditions your stepfamily recognizes. If members are unhappy or unsatisfied with some traditions you've created, respect that. Find out why they feel this way and adjust the traditions accordingly. Remember, the longevity of your stepfamily depends on how well your stepfamily bonds. If stepfamily members feel forced to follow traditions just to please you, then your stepfamily bonding will not be based on honesty. Try to be open to the feelings of your stepfamily members, even if they may feel critical to you. Don't be defensive; that usually breeds deep-seated resentment over time.

How often should you review your stepfamily traditions? Initially, you will need to review them in the first and second years of your plan in order to work out any bugs and to know what works comfortably in your stepfamily. By the third year, you may have reached a comfort level with the traditions you are enjoying in your stepfamily, and I would suggest evaluating every two to three years afterward, not only to be sure your traditions are satisfying to everyone in your stepfamily, but to eliminate those traditions that no longer apply.

The Family Emotional Barometer

One of the most important maintenance tools in your stepfamily will be to check in on each stepfamily member's individual mental health to be sure your stepfamily remains healthy, happy, and content. This is the balance that your stepfamily requires due to the non-related nature of the relationships between you and your stepchild, and the bioparent in the middle.

What is the best way to check on the emotional barometers of your stepfamily members? By reviewing the emotions that your stepfamily members may be experiencing. Once you know the emotions each member is feeling, you can move ahead to know better how to proceed with problem solving.

Exercise: Emotional Check In on Stepfamily Members

Briefly describe your current emotional state at each review of the Stepfamily Plan. Answer the following question.

Stepparent

I feel that the Stepfamily Plan is working because: _____

_____

_____

_____

I feel that our Stepfamily Plan needs work in the following areas:

_____

_____

_____

Bioparent

I feel that the Stepfamily Plan is working because: _____

_____

_____

_____

I feel that our Stepfamily Plan needs work in the following areas:

_____

_____

_____

Stepchild

I feel that the Stepfamily Plan is working because: _____

_____

_____

_____

I feel that our Stepfamily Plan needs work in the following areas:

_____

_____

_____

Whew! You did it. You completed the book and created a positive and workable Stepfamily Plan for your stepfamily. It is my sincerest hope that you found the book helpful and can use it as a future guide for your stepfamily in helping to work through new issues that come up. I wish for each and every one of you a happy, safe, and emotionally secure stepfamily journey into the sometimes unclear and unknown future. Be sure to continue reviewing your Stepfamily Plan for changes in your stepfamily and to identify areas that need continued work. Continue writing in your journal if you feel that would be helpful to you and your stepfamily. Remember to keep the journal for your stepchild as a gift—they may be in a stepfamily someday and you have already done the "legwork" that could help their journey tremendously. Share the book with your stepparent friends and allow them to discover what you did as well as help prevent unnecessary struggles and conflicts in their stepfamilies. Above all, remember to be flexible and open to change in your stepfamily, and welcome each new day in your stepfamily with a gift of thanks to yourself and your stepfamily members for being fortunate enough to live in a very special family that you helped create.

My Stepfamily Journal

Some Other
New Harbinger Titles

The Daughter's-In-Law Survival Guide, Item DSG $12.95

Whose Life Is It Anyway?, Item $14.95

It Happened to Me, Item IHPM $17.95

Act it Out, Item AIO $19.95

Parenting Your Older Adopted Child, Item PYAO $16.95

Boy Talk, Item BTLK $14.95

Talking to Alzheimer's, Item TTA $12.95

Helping a Child with Nonverbal Learning Disorder or Asperger's Syndrome,
Item HCNL $14.95

The 50 Best Ways to Simplify Your Life, Item FWSL $11.95

When Anger Hurts Your Relationship, Item WARY $13.95

The Couple's Survival Workbook, Item CPSU $18.95

Loving Your Teenage Daughter, Item LYTD $14.95

The Hidden Feeling of Motherhood, Item HFM $14.95

Parenting Well When Your Depressed, Item PWWY $17.95

Thinking Pregnant, Item TKPG $13.95

Pregnancy Stories, Item PS $14.95

The Co-Parenting Survival Guide, Item CPSG $14.95

Family Guide to Emotional Wellness, Item FGEW $24.95

How to Survive and Thrive in an Empty Nest, Item NEST $13.95

Children of the Self-Absorbed, Item CSAB $14.95

The Adoption Reunion Survival Guide, Item ARSG $13.95

Undefended Love, Item UNLO $13.95

Why Can't I Be the Parent I Want to Be?, Item PRNT $12.95

Kid Cooperation, Item COOP $14.95

Breathing Room: Creating Space to Be a Couple, Item BR $14.95

Call **toll free, 1-800-748-6273,** or log on to our online bookstore at
www.newharbinger.com to order. Have your Visa or Mastercard number ready.
Or send a check for the titles you want to New Harbinger Publications, Inc., 5674
Shattuck Ave., Oakland, CA 94609. Include $4.50 for the first book and 75¢ for
each additional book, to cover shipping and handling. (California residents please
include appropriate sales tax.) Allow two to five weeks for delivery.

Prices subject to change without notice.